# face2facebook

ArLynn Leiber Presser

# face2facebook

**325 Friends, 365 Days, One Woman's Way of Logging Off and Finding Her Place in the World**

TOWN AND COUNTRY
PUBLIC LIBRARY DISTRICT
320 E. NORTH STREET
ELBURN, IL 60119

TATE PUBLISHING
AND ENTERPRISES, LLC

*Face2Facebook*
Copyright © 2013 by ArLynn Leiber Presser. All rights reserved.

No part of this publication may be reproduced, stored in a retrieval system or transmitted in any way by any means, electronic, mechanical, photocopy, recording or otherwise without the prior permission of the author except as provided by USA copyright law.

The opinions expressed by the author are not necessarily those of Tate Publishing, LLC.

Published by Tate Publishing & Enterprises, LLC
127 E. Trade Center Terrace | Mustang, Oklahoma 73064 USA
1.888.361.9473 | www.tatepublishing.com

Tate Publishing is committed to excellence in the publishing industry. The company reflects the philosophy established by the founders, based on Psalm 68:11,
*"The Lord gave the word and great was the company of those who published it."*

Book design copyright © 2013 by Tate Publishing, LLC. All rights reserved.
*Cover design by Lindsay Behrens*
*Interior design by Mary Jean Archival*

Published in the United States of America

ISBN: 978-1-62563-081-0
1. Biography & Autobiography / Personal Memoirs
2. Travel / Special Interest / Adventure
13.01.11

To my Facebook friends, my "I don't do Facebook"
friends, the new friends and the old,
and, of course, Mark Zuckerberg.

# Contents

December—Friendship: Confirm or Ignore ................. 9

January—Friends 1 through 28: Opening a
    Facebook Account ................................................. 17

February—Friends 29 through 62: Security Settings ... 29

March—Friends 63 through 85: Studied at, Born on,
    Worked at, Hometown ............................................ 45

April—Friends 86–111: Unfriending (Part 1) ............ 59

May—Friends 111 through 141: Basic Info:
    Religious Beliefs ..................................................... 69

June—Friends 142 through 166: Likes ...................... 77

July—Friends 167 through 186: Defriending (Part 2)...89

August—Friends 187 through 206: Activity Recent ... 99

September—Friends 207 through 231: Re-friending .. 107

October—Friends 232 through 246: Add Your
    Current City ......................................................... 117

November—Friends 247 through 268: Deactivation ... 127

December—Friends 269 through 289: Not Just
    Facebook Friends .................................................. 139

Epilogue—Friend 290 ............................................... 147

# December—Friendship: Confirm or Ignore

It happened to me when I turned fifty years old. It will happen to you some time in your life.

Or maybe it already has.

It was the autumn in which I realized that my purpose and meaning were gone.

I was divorced, amicably enough—I always think the people who are bitter about exes reveal a subtle lack of romantic judgment in their very complaints. My two sons had left home—Joseph had taken work in New York, and Eastman decided not to come home from college for summer vacations. I had been a stay-at-home mom, but the house was on the market and was way too large for me both in its size and mortgage payments. My volunteer jobs were being taken over by others—eased out of planning parties and supervising children's fairs. I have no parents that require caregiving, and the two friends for whom I would have cared had passed.

The world had absolutely no need of me.

I could have gotten religion, volunteered at Habitat for Humanity, joined a book club, or bought a cat. A lot of women buy cats.

It might happen to you if you lose your job. Or when your kids leave the nest. Or when you know that you aren't even a supporting player in someone else's lifetime movie, but instead, you're an extra.

I had always been shy, although I think many people who know me would be surprised by that assessment. But I didn't like to go out. Didn't like to meet new people. Got panic attacks at dinner parties, barbecues, and even coffee with friends. Without the ballast of husband and sons, the requirement of sociability, I withdrew. I watched movies online. I went on two-hour walks through the forest preserve. I woke up every morning and thought, *Why am I here?* I read fashion magazines at solitary, leisurely, white-wine lunches.

I tried getting a job, but the two refuges of unskilled women who have been out of the job market—real estate and opening a boutique—didn't look like a great choice in an economy that was quickly disintegrating.

And volunteering? I had directed benefit shows for PTA, constructed booths for antiques shows for the Community House, cooked hot dogs at sidewalk sales to raise money for the Rotary Club, and coached for the Youth Soccer League. I had done all that, and in the end, I was valued exactly what I was paid.

The doctor suggested antidepressants. I declined, mostly because of the expected weight gain. As invisible as I was to the world, a fat fifty-year-old woman is even more invisible.

And besides, I wasn't depressed. I wasn't isolated. I had a rich and varied social life. Most of it in my pajamas. I logged on to Facebook, and there I was—watching videos that friends found too cute not to share, liking photos of friends' children, commenting "I'm so sorry" when a friend announced the passing of a mother or pet turtle.

I got friend requests from ex-boyfriends who followed up with lengthy apologies, dissections, and explanations—as if a quarter century hadn't passed. These often ended with a wistful "I'm married now, with two beautiful children, but it's not really a marriage."

I got friend requests from classmates from high school, college, law school. A flurry of reminiscences and a catch-up on the years—and then a lingering worry that I've gotten this person confused with someone else. Maybe this person didn't actually sit behind me in math class.

I got friend requests from people who recognized my name—my grandfather was the science fiction writer Fritz Leiber—and so I had all sorts of friends around the world. These friends often had the most interesting posts and played the best games—Mafia Wars, Farmville, Ninjas versus Pirates, Sorority Sisters.

I had a sense I could build an entire life around Facebook if I could just persuade the Domino's pizza delivery guy to pick up beer on the way to my house.

I sent friend requests to everybody Facebook suggested. And so I was friends with one of the cashiers at the grocery store where I shopped. But not with any of the others. And only with one bag boy. I was Facebook friends with the photography store in town even though I never went there, and besides, the owner didn't like me in real life. I was friends with everybody that Facebook suggested as in "people you may know" and sometimes I thought "wait, I know we have friends in common but who is this person?"

I sent friendship requests to my biological father and mother who had given me up for adoption when I was three years old. My father—Justin Leiber—accepted. My mother—Aleta Clayton—ignored my request, which is Facebook code for "forget it!"

I sent a friendship request to my cousin whom I hadn't seen since I participated in an intervention. Her parting words to me at the time had been "you jerk." Now she owned a stationery store in Rhode Island, and we messaged back and forth in a cautious way. I always thought of her as the most glamorous gal around and still did.

My ex-husband Stephen joined Facebook, and we were friends for exactly twenty-four hours before deciding it was better not to know what the other was doing. Oddly, I was Facebook friends with his girlfriend. And later, with the girlfriend's new husband who became her ex-husband and who had three mutual friends with me. Facebook makes all of us into Kevin Bacon with just a few degrees of separation. In fact, Facebook recently announced that its users are, on average, just four degrees away from any other user.

I became Facebook friends with a foster sister from a home I had lived in when I was a teenager.

"Did you have sex with my dad?" she messaged me.

"Yes, and I regret it," I said. "He said that if I didn't, he'd have me sent to another placement, and I wouldn't be able to finish school."

"I knew you two were doing it. I hated him. He's in Hell now."

Out of guilt, I followed up by liking several of her links to internet comics she wrote.

My sons came home for Christmas. I made Christmas luncheon which included Stephen, his first ex-wife, my stepdaughter Elisabeth, her husband Steve, and their daughter Grace. The easiest conversation opener was the latest series of videos of Grace that Elisabeth had posted on Facebook.

And then, everybody went home. The boys went out with friends. I was in front of the computer with my Facebook friends and family. I was in my pajamas. I had a glass of champagne next to the mouse pad. There was something wrong with me that I felt more at ease, less anxious, less self-conscious in this pretend world that now was exploding with Merry Christmas posts with links to YouTube videos of carolers and photos of family pets beside a decorated tree.

I thought back to earlier in December. I really had to check in on Mark Cage.

I play Scrabble on Facebook. If you can't find a partner among your friends, Facebook will match you up with someone. Sometimes you play a game, and that's the end of it. Sometimes you play a game, and you start to chat online while you're playing. Then, you send a friend request. And then, you play more scrabble.

Mark was that kind of Facebook friend. I knew he taught school somewhere in England, that he was a runner, that he had a daughter who lived with her mother in Turkey, and that he probably liked to play Scrabble with me because he always won. While playing in early December, a message from him popped up on my screen.

> Mark: I'm really feeling depressed. We just broke up, and I'm devastated.

I didn't know who "her" was, but I quickly replied.

> Me: I'm sorry. What happened?

> Mark: She flew over from Sweden. I had met her playing Worlds of Warcraft. But all she wanted to do was sit on the couch and play video games.

> Me: Is she back in Sweden?

> Mark: Yeah. I just don't think I'm ever going to be in a relationship again. I don't see how I'll stop from making the same mistakes again and again. I'm worried about myself and what I might do.

We played and chatted online. Maybe he felt safe to vent with me, and I was truly worried about him. When he said he needed to turn in, I suggested a game the next day. We played three days in a row, and while the actual word *suicide* never came up, I was uneasy. Texts are an imperfect communication tool and I could have been overreacting.

> Mark: For the first time in my life, I'm really thinking about it.

> Me: You can't because of your daughter.

> Mark: I don't get to see her except for in the summer. My ex would be happy I'm sure.

> Me: You can never let your daughter grow up knowing you did this.

I had thought about it too. One of those terrifically smart, sophisticated, and somber French philosophers wrote that whether to kill one's self or not is the first and most important question. If so, I was asking the most important question every morning. I had wanted to, sometimes I still wanted to, but I would never because of Joseph and Eastman. I figure I have made them crazy enough without adding on "my mom committed suicide."

I was relieved when Mark logged on in what was for him the late evening and for me the mid-afternoon. We chatted, and I didn't mind when he won. And then, even before I could send a congratulations, he would start the next game. Why did I care? But was I really so much of a good person that I wanted to be of comfort to someone I had never met and would never meet?

No. I'm pretty sure the answer is no.

The answer is that I wanted to feel needed, to have purpose, to be a friend who was important to another friend.

On the fourth day, we played just a few rounds. No chatting until…

> Mark: I'm going out with some of the lads for a pint. Have a great night!

We'd play again. He'd beat me at Scrabble. I'd comment on photos he'd take on field trips with his students.

On Christmas day, I realized I had 324 Facebook friends. I clicked on Friends List and scrolled down. Some of the names were familiar, some made me pause, some I saw every day but only knew what was going on because I read their Facebook posts, some I hadn't seen in decades, and a few I couldn't place at all.

Who *are* these people? I wondered.

Who were the friends who would take my weepy call at 2:00 a.m.? Who were the friends I could count on when I was sick? Who were the ones who would go to the movies with me? Keep all my secrets? Cherish my successes and help me recover from defeats? Really, who were they? And who was I with a vast social life that didn't require me to get out of bed? I had often struggled with getting out of the house, meeting people, facing the world. Was I hiding on Facebook?

# January—Friends 1 through 28: Opening a Facebook Account

According to my timeline, I opened a Facebook account in March 2007.

Stephen and I separated when I was in my midforties. He bought a condominium downtown and he stayed there during the week. On weekends, he moved back into our house, and I sublet a basement apartment in the city. We wanted to avoid making Joseph and Eastman into the kind of children of divorce who have to pack everything they own into a backpack every weekend.

The neighborhood where I stayed on weekends was a tense mix of Hassidic Jews and Muslims from Pakistan and India. I didn't feel comfortable being outside by myself. And no matter how many times I talked to the landlord, the back door of the apartment was secured not by a lock but by duct tape, and the kitchen ceiling had collapsed so that I could see the pipes and beams and insulation—the place where hordes of rats and creepy, crawling things might emerge. Still, it was a cheap place to live for one and a half days a week.

Every Saturday afternoon, I packed up and moved to the apartment—stopping at the grocery for provisions. I locked myself into the bedroom and put a chair up under the doorknob. And then, I would settle down with my computer. The neighbors upstairs had unsecured wireless. And I had until Monday morning.

I wasn't lonely. I shopped at Amazon, kept up with celebrities at TMZ, looked for work on craigslist, wrote long e-mails to everybody I knew. One Saturday, my friend Lanny Jones e-mailed that I should read an online magazine article about Facebook. The article warned parents about the possibility of predators. The thing about raising children is somebody is always warning you about predators, and since I was already ruining my kids' lives by getting a divorce, I had to at least make sure they weren't ever at the mercy of predators.

And besides, Lanny had been once been an editor at People magazine. Surely, he knew what was trending.

I opened up a Facebook account. It was easy. I even managed to add a picture. I sent friendship requests to my sons Joseph and Eastman and looked at their profiles. Eastman had over four hundred friends. I started looking at each of his friends' profiles to make sure they were friends from school, from camp, from bands he had played in. Absolutely no predators.

I posted on his wall that I hoped he had a good time that weekend.

Within minutes, Eastman called me—he almost never called me on the weekends.

"If you're going to be my Facebook friend, you can't ever comment on my page," he said.

"And hello to you too."

"In fact, I don't even want you *looking* at my page," he said.

"Okay, fine, agreed."

After he hung up, I went back to trolling through his friends. He hadn't thought to tell me I couldn't do that.

And then a little red number 2 appeared at the top of the screen next to the word *Facebook*. I hesitated. Clicking on a new link, opening an unfamiliar file, replying to e-mails from anybody asking for a social security number—I wasn't born yesterday, those things were all dangerous. So of course, I clicked on the little red number.

A friendship request. Lanny wanted to be my friend. All I had to do was confirm. Lanny had his own Facebook account and now we were friends. I also had a friendship request from William Clark. William Clark had been a nineteenth century explorer and officer in the US army. He was dead. I opened up my Hotmail account and e-mailed Lanny. After all, Lanny had written a biography of Clark.

Me: You have a Facebook account for a dead guy?

Lanny: Yes. And you can message him on Facebook. Click on the middle icon. This is the future, and you are too young to have a Hotmail account.

I started looking up everybody I knew and sending them friendship requests. Every time I logged on, Facebook recommended friends. And I was getting friendship requests—every time I saw a red number hovering over the friends icon I felt noticed, fun, and popular. Sometimes, I didn't know who people were, but I felt like I'd be rude to say no. But now I really had something to do on weekends to pass the hours until Monday.

I hadn't locked myself into a basement apartment in a sketchy neighborhood because I didn't know what to do with myself.

No, I was at a big party where I didn't have to dress up.

Over the course of the latter part of 2010, I thought more about these friends. The friends I would never see again or maybe never meet at all. I went out on my walks through the town. I thought about what I would be like if I were not scared of planes, travel, people, being outside of my house, terrorists, tornadoes, car crashes, panic attacks, and five hundred assorted other things. And as many of us do as we approach the New Year, I thought about how I could be a different person with just the right resolution.

I could resolve to lose five pounds. I wanted to look pretty; who doesn't? And pretty would mean the possibility of romance, of love, of a new life.

I could resolve to quit drinking. White wine kept me company almost every night. Especially when I felt invisible, rejected, purposeless—a cold chardonnay could fool me into thinking that the best days were just ahead.

I could resolve to be more organized.

But I had made those three resolutions every year, and by February, I was still 138 pounds, I was still asking Mr. Alcohol to make me feel better, and the hall closet still had no room for coats and umbrellas.

For New Years' Eve of 2011, I was invited—yippee! And do I have to go?—to a sedate suburban white elephant party. A guest was required to wrap a present they had received at Christmas, something they didn't like.

The party would include roast beef, an elaborate cake, a glass of champagne at midnight, an exchange of the reject presents, and I'd be home by twelve thirty—in time to stay up all night, hoping Eastman came home safely. I was going with Charlie, and he was halfway dressed for the party when I stopped by his apartment. I told him about my New Year's Resolution while he brushed his hair. He was a man who made a tuxedo look good.

"I just want to meet them all, every one of them, in person."

"It's going to be impossible, but I think trying it sounds like a blast!"

"Maybe it will be a blast, but mostly, I just want to know which of my friends are real and which are just on facebook."

He held up a selection of bow ties. I pointed to the red one, and he gave it to me.

"Why do you think it's impossible?" I added "And by the way, I'm not completely sure I'm going to do this."

"I think you'd find this hard because you'd have to get on a plane, which you don't like to do. But it's not just you. It's that you'd have to have everybody's cooperation. Impossible."

"Lift your chin. I could do this. I will do this."

"What are you going to do if you fly to, say, India and the friend stands you up?"

"I'll cry."

"All right, I've got to find my cuff links. You want to post it on Facebook? You could even do it as a video."

"I don't know how to make a video."

"Lady, lady, lady—this is why you have me in your life. Just sit in front of the computer. Look at the circle right there."

"I won't be able to walk Eddie for you. Because I'll be on the road. A lot. We won't be able to see each other very much. Wow, that's a lens? I always wondered what that was."

I sat down at his computer, and it was a little like looking in a mirror. I pulled at the loose skin along my jawline, wondering for not the first time what I'd look like if I got just a little work done.

"All right, start talking," Charlie said.

And so I did. While Charlie looked for his cuff links.

He edited the video which is truly what he's gifted at. We posted it and went to the party. I ended up with a goldfish that would die the next day. Charlie came away with something that looked like a Frisbee or a flying saucer, but it was actually supposed to exercise one's abs.

"Can I just delete that video?" I asked when he dropped me back at the house.

"I guess. Probably nobody's seen it. Everybody is out at a party."

"Sorry. I know you put some effort into it."

The house was empty and quiet. Upstairs, I took off my dress and flipped open my laptop. I'd delete the video and check on my friends. Eastman and Joseph wouldn't be home for hours.

I got into my pajamas, tucked myself in under the covers and logged on.

It was worse and better than I had imagined.

Twenty-eight comments on my post. All of them invitations. Fourteen likes. And a picture posted on my page of a dead roasted pig—with a cheerful New Year's greeting and a promise from Del Rosario Bitanga that when I came to the Philippines, his entire village would host a party for me with presumably a fresher pig.

Who was Mark? Why was I friends with what looked to be a twentysomething Filipino? I scrolled through his profile page and then noticed that he listed my grandfather Fritz Leiber as one of his likes. Okay, now I remembered—he was into science fiction and wrote fantasy comic books. I had even contacted Fritz's agent on his behalf because he wanted an American publisher.

On the hook to fly to the Philippines. I felt a funny clutch in my chest.

And then there was Warner Sills whose best friend had worked on a student film with Eastman. The three of us—Warner, his friend, and I—had had lunch together. Followed up with a friendship request. Which led to the occasional exchange of messages and finally…nothing. We hadn't communicated in more than a year. Warner posted a message saying that he didn't live in Chicago anymore, he was in graduate school in Taipei.

Who had given Warner permission to move to Taipei?

Maybe I could parse this out with a lawyerly precision: only friends within the United States. My New Year's Resolution was that I was only going to see friends in the United States.

But then, there was the friendship request notification. A woman named Julianne Couch who tendered a friendship request because our mutual friend Lanny Jones had told her about my resolution at a New Year's Eve party they both attended.

"I live in Wyoming," she wrote in the message accompanying her friendship request. "But I'm moving to Iowa, which will be a lot closer and easier, so don't come see me until June."

What if more people friended me? What was I supposed to do about that?

The snow was coming down quietly, one flake after another, a thick blanket on the yard. The house was empty and Eastman would most likely send me a text saying he was staying over at someone's house, Joseph would too. Responsible choices for young adults at a New Year's party.

I could take down the post. But there would be people who would remember this—jeez, one of them who had taken the time to get a picture of a dead pig up on my wall.

I could put up a second post saying that the first post was a prank devised by someone who had figured out my password. Way too elaborate.

The screen in front of me popped with notifications. More people liking and commenting and sending me message and I thought, *What kind of loser spends New Year's Eve on Facebook?*

And the answer, of course, was that I was that loser. The fifty-year-old gal with her night cream and pajamas on, drinking champagne out of a Styrofoam cup in an empty house. And all around the world, people just like me were logging in, commenting, liking, sharing links and photos and gripes and delights. My peeps.

I had taken the safest place in the world—my desk, the computer, Facebook—and had suggested I would turn it into a roiling pit of airplane travel, meeting new people, going to places in the world that I had only read about in books. There was such a potential for disaster, for damage, for death. There was everything I had anxiety attacks considering.

I could deactivate the account. Leave Facebook entirely. It was a time suck. I could do something productive. Although I felt a bit vague about what would constitute productive. I had not felt productive in a long time.

I could do this resolution. Three hundred twenty-four friends. Okay, 325 if you count Lanny's friend from Wyoming. Three hundred sixty-five days. A friend a day. I should forget completely about overseas. If I put that part of the job in the secret compartment lockbox of my brain where I wouldn't actually think about it, this sort of sounded fun. I would certainly have a reason to get up every morning. I had a little savings set aside. I wasn't sure it was going to cover everything, but if I made a good faith effort and ran out of money, my Facebook friends would understand if I couldn't finish.

And maybe Warner would come back to the United States.

I opened a WordPress account. I wanted to keep a record of what I was doing. I googled where to buy a flip video camera. Online, it looked like the best camera for dummies. I sent replies to every message and post. I opened a package of index cards and, with one name per card, tried to organize where these friends were from.

Every time I thought too much about what I was doing, I just told myself I was testing whether it was possible. I always had the deactivation option. But I had a general idea that this resolution was possible for someone who was organized and unafraid. Organized I could fake. I went to bed just as the sun came up, thinking that *if* I was going to do this, I knew how I would have to do it. A friend a day, grouping friends by geography, making up time so that in the future that I wouldn't think about too much, I would go to a pig roast.

"Are you friends with all my ex-girlfriends?" Eastman asked me on the morning of January 3.

"Just Katie and Dana. And Leslie."

"It's weird."

"Some of your girlfriends have sent me requests when you're together. I didn't think I could defriend them when you break up. It seemed rude."

"Okay, well, Katie sent me a text. You're meeting all your Facebook friends?"

"I think so."

"What are you going to do with these people when you meet them?"

"I guess anything they want to do as long as it's not illegal or immoral. Renee, the barista from Caribou?

She's a hairdresser on the side. She's going to braid my hair."

"You mean like dreads?"

"Sort of."

I was used to the look he gave me.

"You're my Facebook friend," I pressed.

"You either got to drive me back to school," he said. "Or we have to do something now because Dad's coming to pick me up in an hour to take me back."

"What do you want to do?" I asked. "And by the way, I'm going to blog about it."

"I'm going to go smoke a cigarette on the front porch."

He went outside. I had been pretty lucky with Eastman and Joseph on the whole "drugs, drinking, and generally getting into trouble" thing that teenagers put their parents through just so that their parents will be ashamed of what they put their own parents through. I chose my battles, and smoking wasn't going to be one of them. In fact, I had smoked cigarettes with him before—generally, when we were getting over an argument.

I went out on the porch. We smoked two cigarettes each. I filmed him and me together. Four takes for a minute-long video talking about being facebook friends. I knew I couldn't edit like Charlie, but I could document that I had actually done it. I had met my first Facebook friend. Face-to-face. Even if it was my own kid and it was on the front porch. I had proof that it had happened.

My ex-husband's two-seater pulled into the driveway.

"Okay, I gotta go," Eastman said, and he ground out his cigarette on the steps and gave me a hug.

Stephen got out of the car and walked up to the porch.

Eastman slipped past me with his backpack and suitcase, which he threw into the trunk.

I stood on the porch until the car pulled out onto the street. I considered getting a cup of coffee, a magazine, and an hour on the treadmill. But I had a video to upload—or at least, to learn how to upload—on my brand-new blog. And I had something to write about. And then I should figure out which Facebook friend I could see next. I needed to make plans. I had 362 days left in the year.

"Just 324 more friends and I'm done," I said, feeling far too proud of myself. I would definitely get humbled.

# February—Friends 29 through 62: Security Settings

In January, Renee came to put in corn rows which hurt a whole lot. I weight trained with a friend of my older son Joseph. I learned that boxing is way more strategy than brawn. Although brawn helps. I painted fishnets on my stepdaughter's daughter, ate two horseshoes (and heartburn) in a single day, and got a temporary tramp stamp with the Nepalese translation of my name. I spent an afternoon coloring paper dolls with a woman ten years my senior and got the full court sales pitch for Reliv energy and diet products. All with Facebook friends.

I learned about butterfly cultivation, the dating habits of teenage girls, the struggles of a "cub" lifestyle, selective mutism, and how working at Target is even more depressing than I had imagined it was. I went to a food pantry with a friend and learned how to apply for food stamps.

I heard five intersecting stories of divorce, adultery, and cocaine from five Facebook friends.

I recorded everything on video—except who was sleeping with whom. But I had the butterflies, the weight training, the tramp stamp, and even a Facebook friend bursting into tears as he talked about losing his job. I had my own weepy videos. I uploaded and blogged and plotted out trips that took me all over Illinois. I had no boring friends; it was just a matter of figuring out what they were passionate about, what interested them, what mattered, what their purpose was.

There were the lost days. Days when I would pick up a magazine, a bottle of wine, and a bag of Skinny Pop at the grocery store. And it would be nine o'clock before I'd realize that I had done nothing of substance except established that the return of the palazzo pant was imminent.

But there were fewer lost days than there had been before January because I had to blog every day or I felt like I was falling behind. Because I was meeting with friends. Because I was dividing the country into geographic zones and sending out messages that began with "Hey, friend, I have a special New Year's resolution and I need your help."

Because I had meaning and purpose and fervor. Even if it was silly and not likely to do anything to better the world, and sometimes, people were utterly baffled when I explained what I was trying to do. I ignored the gnawing sense that there were better things to do with my time because of course, there were, but I had not made much headway on doing those better things. I ignored the people who said I was an idiot, that it was impossible to see this many people in one year, that said Facebook was silly, that said I would freak the first time I had to get on a plane.

I never ignored this question: aren't you worried about all the crazies out there?

Just like online, I had my own personal security settings: I never met someone for the first time unless it was in a public place. I often posted that I was on my way to meet a particular friend, and I figured that if the friend went nuts, killed me, and disposed of my body parts in the forest preserve, there were 324 Facebook friends who knew exactly who did it.

And I started looking for chaperones.

I planned a first big trip around seven Facebook friends. I had gone to college with Dale who now lived in Atlanta, Georgia, with his family. Brenda Allison was a lawyer from the city—she had moved with her husband to Fayetteville, Arkansas. I had met Sarah Loeffel Roberts from Palm Harbour, Florida, only once, at a wedding. I had been so anxious that I couldn't remember much about her, but she had sent me a friendship request the next day, so I must not have been too awful. There was Sammie Scruggs whom I had never met and wasn't quite sure why we knew each other, but he lived in Huntsville, Alabama, where my Scrabble buddy Jonathan Boyd now lived. That made Huntsville a twofer.

My biological father Justin lived in Tallahassee, and he was my Facebook friend. I could fly in to see him. Then I could use Tallahassee as a hub for Atlanta, Fayetteville, Huntsville, Palm Harbour. It would be a five-day, six-friend operation with its base in Tallahassee. It would require long hours in a rental car and two flights.

During the day, when I plotted and planned, it seemed genius.

When I woke up in the middle of the night, it seemed like the stupidest and most dangerous thing I would ever do.

Surely, the trip would end with a fatal plane crash, a heart attack while driving, bee sting induced anaphylactic shock, a snakebite, a long howling scream of anxiety, and the possibility of being murdered.

That last possibility convinced me I needed a chaperone.

I had met Reggie only once when we had both helped out a mutual friend on an amateur music video. I had written the script and sat in on the filming. Reggie had flown in to be part of the cast—he was an army captain, but he had occasionally dabbled in acting. Everybody who had worked on that video became Facebook friends with everyone else. In January, Reggie was stationed in Savannah. And I remembered he had grown up in Huntsville. I called him.

"I'd buy you a plane ticket to Tallahassee. And then we'd drive up to Huntsville. I have two friends I have to see. You make sure I'm safely back at whatever hotel we stay at, and you go off and spend time with your friends and family."

"Who are you friends with in Huntsville?"

"Jonathan Boyd and Sammie Scruggs."

"How are you friends with Sammie?"

"I've been trying to figure that out."

"He's my cousin. And he does that all the time—becoming friends with everybody on my friends list."

"He'll be happy to see us both."

I confessed that I had never before bought an airline ticket on my own, and Reggie said he'd take care of arrangements for both of us.

"Didn't you know this is what I do, what my job is?"

## Face2Facebook

I didn't know what he did in the army except that when he was stationed in Iraq, I would send him care packages on the same schedule as my sons. In fact, I sort of thought of him as a son. Now that he was back in the States, his Facebook page made it look like his patriotic obligations were to go to Prince concerts and get his picture taken with beautiful women who were going to catch their death of cold if they didn't put on a sweater.

Reggie would turn out to be the only thing that went right with the trip.

My father Justin and I played Scrabble on Facebook, and he usually won. We had a more complicated relationship outside of Facebook. He and my mother Aleta put me up for adoption when I was three years old. I was twenty-five when I hired a detective to find them. I was his daughter, but I was not part of the family. Justin was not really part of my family—the boys had probably met him less than a dozen times. My half-sister Casey lived just a few blocks away from my son Joseph in New York and they were both in their early twenties. But despite my nagging Joseph to call her, they never spoke.

My project would change that. Justin had prostate cancer which had now metastasized. This might be one of our last chances to forge a good relationship.

A few days before the trip, I had logged on in the morning and noticed that Justin had posted six status updates in the course of an hour. Read together, it was an angry diatribe against sexual mores, Republicans, Catholics and people who don't understand Socrates.

Maybe it was intellectually advanced. Or maybe it was crazy talk. Either was possible.

A few hours later I got a call from my half-sister Casey.

"Did you see the posts?"

"Yeah," I said. "They seem a bit incomprehensible."

"It's embarrassing. He doesn't seem to realize that it's a public post. Anybody can see it. In fact, the way I found out about it is that one of my friends called me. They saw it this morning. I made him give me his password and I took the posts down."

"Okay. He's a philosophy professor. Maybe this was somehow very intellectual and we just don't get it."

"Please! He's going crazy. He's been taking some medication that is making him psychotic. I am going to fly down and see you when we get there. Maybe we can get him to stop taking this drug."

The morning of the flight to Tallahassee, I mentally said "good-bye, farewell forever!" to the flower shop, the park, the grocery store as the cab drove me to the airport. Once there, I was surrounded by competent world travelers who knew what they were doing. I was pulled out of the line for random screening, and as the TSA agent ran her hands over my body, I knew everybody else in the airport was thinking, *She looks like a terrorist to me*!

I went directly to the airport bar and ordered a beer. I could only assume that everybody else at the bar—including the couple eating huevos rancheros and drinking the largest margaritas I have ever seen—were from a different time zone where it was 5:00 p.m.

Somewhere in the middle of the Atlantic.

I went to the gate and boarded a plane full of relaxed travelers who played games on their cell phones and concentrated on their paperbacks. I texted Joseph "I love you" so that the last message he ever received from me would have sufficient gravitas. I did the same for Eastman.

The cabin door closed. My last opportunity for escape. I wanted out. I could get up and make a fuss. I'd be a headline on Fox news, but I could do it.

But I didn't. I tried to be like the other passengers who turned off their cell phones when the flight attendants demanded. The other passengers who closed their eyes and leaned their heads back as we catapulted down the runway. The other passengers who calmly crossed their arms over their chests. I rocked back and forth and realized that I was doing so in the exact same rhythm as the woman next to me.

When Justin picked me up at the airport, I knew immediately that I couldn't go off with Reggie to Huntsville or go anywhere else. Justin seemed to have completely forgotten about matters such as lane usage, stoplights, and why a driver should use a turn signal. He also got lost. He had forgotten about the give and take of conversation. He had lost the ability to clip the wire between thought and voice—there was no shutting him up. Plato, sodomy, politics, a memory sparked by whatever was on the road, it was like his brain had opened up the levees and everything was rushing out.

"I don't understand what you're talking about," I said. "Could you slow down? The car, that is."

But he hardly noticed me. Or traffic. At his apartment, he switched to the conspiracy against him, and it was huge—including virtually all of the employees of the university and many of his doctors.

"They want me to stop taking Ropinirole," he ranted. "It's the only thing that controls my shaking. Which is a side effect of the Taxatere I take for my prostate cancer. But if I can't stop shaking, I can't work, I can't do anything. Effectively, they want me to die. That's what they want. But I'm not going to let them."

He continued to talk as he stood outside the bathroom as I peed. And later, when I barricaded myself in Casey's bedroom, he shouted outside the door well past 3:00 a.m. When I woke up at seven he was waiting at the dining room table. Talking even before I opened the bedroom door.

He said he was going to dress to go to his office. I excused myself to the bathroom I opened the medicine cabinet and pulled out the medications. No Ropinirole. But I wasn't surprised—if I was the target of a vast conspiracy to get me to not take Ropinirole I wouldn't leave it in the medicine cabinet.

Taxatere, Bupropion, Xanax, Wellbutrin.

All filled at the same pharmacy. I called.

"I'm Justin Leiber's daughter. You've been filling his prescriptions for a while and this past week you filled one for Ropinirole. It was a prescription from his general doctor. But his oncologist is prescribing Taxatere for his prostate cancer. I'm wondering about drug interaction issues."

"I can't talk about a customer. There's a confidentiality problem."

"Okay, but as a general matter."

"As a general matter, those two drugs together often have an interaction that results in an induced psychosis."

"Did you tell him this would happen when you filled the prescription?"

"Yes. I mean I'm not talking to you."

"Okay, I'll just take this to mean I've walked into Crazytown and Justin's the mayor."

I walked out into the living room. Justin was looking for his keys.

"Where's the Ropinirole?" I asked.

"You're part of them. You want me to die."

"No, I just wanted to make sure you had it with you."

We walked to his office on campus. There was no need for me to talk, and besides, there was no room between his words for mine. I felt a rising panic.

"Look at these photographs," he said. "You can tell a lot about a man by what pictures he keeps in his office, so I'm going to talk to you about each one of these pictures and what each one means to me. Now this one..."

I did a quick calculation during the fifteen minutes devoted to a picture of Justin as a young man seated beside Noam Chomskey. With thirty-two pictures and a quarter of an hour devoted to each picture, I would be here for eight hours. The torrent of words was not going to stop.

Justin's pictures destroyed me. Pictures in his office might say a lot about him, and what they said was that

I was not a part of his life. Neither were my two sons. I had fooled myself many times over the years, thinking I meant something to him. I didn't. So what was I doing in Tallahassee?

I didn't mean anything to him. I didn't mean anything to a lot of people. Why had I chosen a project that would remind me of this?

My chest hurt, I couldn't breathe, I went to the bathroom and cried. It was a two-Ativan panic attack and fifteen minutes before I could return to his office. By then, he had forgotten about the photographs. We walked around the campus; he wanted to show me where he taught his seminar, and then he pissed his pants.

"It's okay," he said. "It's been happening—I think it's a side effect."

"Well, let's get you home."

"I don't need to go home."

So we walked through the campus, passing people who quickly looked away when they registered the dark spill all over his pants. He wanted to stop for lunch at a favorite deli. I pleaded that I needed to use the computer first. At the apartment, Justin changed his clothes and talked the entire time I sat at the dining room table and then, as he changed his clothes, shouting from the bedroom.

Casey came into town that afternoon and, as we sat together in the dining room, Justin allowed her to interrupt him.

"You have to stop taking the Ropinirole."

"You're with them."

"With who?"

Justin looked at me.

"The conspiracy," I said. "You're part of the conspiracy."

At the airport the next day, I offered Reggie two hundred dollars, the entire contents of my wallet.

"I'll drop you off at the nearest strip club, library, coffee shop, bar, whatever," I said. "You don't want to be around my dad right now. The trip's a disaster."

"ArLynn, I didn't come here for your dad. Or your project. Or—"

"I could give you money to rent a car, and you could drive by yourself up to Huntsville to see Sammie."

"I didn't come here even to see my cousin. I came here for you."

It was a touching moment, one that would have made me cry or hug him or say something sentimental. But I saw over his shoulder that Justin had gotten out of the car and had approached some people on the sidewalk. He was talking with them. Maybe *with* is the wrong word. They had the look of people who have just discovered that they were going to be given a bonus to their air travel experience—a lecture on Plato or Epictetus or Kierkegaard from a man who had just pissed his pants.

"Get in the car, Justin," I ordered as I slid past him into the driver's seat.

We took turns sitting with Justin. Casey tried to persuade him to stop taking the Ropinirole and she became visibly upset when he would accuse her of being part of the conspiracy between Barbara and the doctors.

Reggie employed the strategy of watching football with the sound off and letting Justin provide the commentary about ancient Greek philosophers and his prostate, politics, and his wife's treason. When he learned that Reggie was in the army, Justin disgorged every fact and theory of military history he had in his brain, not realizing that Reggie was a graduate of West Point and had forgotten more about military history than Justin had ever learned. I tried to be quiet, but occasionally I would try to say something. It was always a mistake.

Casey and Reggie flew out on Monday. I told Casey I wanted to be a better sister to her. I hadn't grown up with her. I hadn't been part of her life. But I had seen how caring she was towards Justin. And sweet.

"You want to go on another trip, I'll go," Reggie said. "You were talking about Mexico City. I'll go. Army sends me all kinds of places but I don't get to see much."

"You got to see the inside of an apartment in Tallahassee."

I could have said, "I couldn't have done this without you," and maybe I did and I just don't remember the words. But I at least remember we hugged good-bye and Reggie went through the TSA line. I went back to the apartment.

Justin's mood had soured. I was now part of the conspiracy and maybe even the head of it. I was only too happy when it was time to go to the airport on Tuesday. Justin barely acknowledged my exit.

Downstairs, I asked the building manager where I could go for a cab to the airport.

"Oh, just let me take you," she said. "I'm actually heading that way because it's my lunch break. Have a seat and I'll get my car out of the garage."

And I sat down on the upholstered sofa.

Justin charged into the lobby.

"I figured out what you are," he snarled. "You're a super conman! It takes a thief to catch a thief, and I've caught you out. I knew when you lied yesterday about Reggie. There's no such thing as a commander in the Army."

"He told me he is being promoted to commander," I said uneasily. I looked out to the parking garage. Where was the building manager? She had said it was not worth calling a cab to the Tallahassee airport. It was so close. She'd drive me. I could just sit in the lobby until she got her car.

"Commander is a Navy term," Justin said. "There's no such rank in the Army."

He was standing nearly on top of me, shaking his prosecutor's finger at me. This is what happens when you confront the leader of the conspiracy, I thought. I kicked my bag toward the door to the parking garage.

"We went through this yesterday. Remember, you made me read the definition in the dictionary? It said that in the Army, you could be a commander, but it's not a rank, it's a term that means leader."

"Admit it. Admit it, Goddamnit, he's not in the Army. You brought him into my house because—"

I stood up.

"You're a super conman and you've disabled my car."

He shoved me. Hard. Up against the wall next to the door to the parking garage. His chest butting up against my forearm. I brought my shoulder up to protect my face.

You can't really shoved back at a seventy-two-year-old man who is shorter, battling cancer, who might or might not have remembered to pull on a diaper, so shoving him back might make him piss himself and then there'd be a mess. Oh, and who's tripping on a Ropinirole?

His car was in the parking garage, a Volkswagon that I could have pointed out to him had trouble starting all weekend.

"You just like Reggie because you like black—"

I can't write the word he used. So I'll just jump ahead to the part where I saw the building manager's car. Justin saw her too, just as she pulled up to the curb. He beat me to opening the door to the garage.

"Mr. Leiber," she said, leaning her head out the driver's side window. "Is anything the matter?"

He yanked at the driver's side door twice before it opened.

"My car won't start. It's her. She's a super conman. And she brought that black man into our house because—"

"That nice young man?" The building manager looked at me. "I thought he was your son."

I shrugged.

"She disabled my car," Justin snarled.

"Do you want me to call the service like I did last week?"

Justin let go of the door handle, lifting up his shoulders with imperial grace.

"I *want* you to have this woman arrested."

The building manager was Polish, about my age, and she made a rapid calculation.

"Get in the car."

I threw my bag across the hood of the car and caught it as it slid off the passenger side, ripping my skirt on the fender. Justin had pulled the driver's side door open again.

"Don't drive her anywhere. She's dangerous! She's a super conman!"

That last part was a scream that faded as she pulled into traffic. The manager and I both managed to shut our doors before we turned off Monroe Street.

*Wow. Great. The last time I see my dad, and I'm going to remember that it's like this*, I thought.

"He's not always like this," she said. "I haven't seen you here, so I don't know how often you see him."

"I think he came to visit me in Chicago four years ago. But we're Facebook friends. We mostly play Scrabble. You can do that on Facebook. Scrabble."

We had stopped at the intersection. She stared at me. Maybe deciding whether she had made a mistake.

"I made a New Year's resolution," I said. "To meet all my Facebook friends. Reggie—the black guy that you thought was my son—he's my Facebook friend too."

"Huh."

She drove for several minutes before asking, "How many Facebook friends do you have?"

"Three hundred and twenty-five. And Justin and Reggie, they were the thirtieth and thirty-second friends I've seen this year. And my sister Casey is 31. You saw her yesterday. It's February, so I was roughly on target. The light's changed. I thought I could figure out who my friends are, what my life is, how I can manage in the world."

She shrugged as if this made perfect sense, as if she had once done this sort of thing herself, as if—no, no—she didn't think I was just as crazy as Justin. She asked me only one more question and that was "What airline?" I was too weary to make small talk. I'm going to die in a fiery plane crash, and I don't care if it's eleven thirty in the morning, *I'm going to have a preflight beer*, I thought. Why the hell didn't I resolve to lose five pounds and stop drinking like I do every year? And then, I could fail with a twelfth night white wine and pasta bender instead of this.

She pulled the car up to the United terminal.

"You're going to have an interesting year," she said.

"Thank you for the ride," I said. "And no, I think this is sort of done for me."

I got out of the car, got my ticket from the kiosk, and headed for security, thinking that I didn't care whether the plane crashed, and maybe it's a better idea for some relationships to stay just friends on Facebook.

The resolution was over. I had put off failure long enough.

# March—Friends 63 through 85: Studied at, Born on, Worked at, Hometown

On Facebook, everybody is having a better time than you are.

On LinkedIn, they have better jobs—no, wait, careers.

On MySpace, they're listening to better music. On Twitter, they're doing everything you're doing but it's like they've had four Red Bulls.

Facebook is supposed to be how we keep in touch. How we share good times and milestones. How we find that person we went to high school with and compare how we've done since. How we figure out whether our ex has moved on with that guy she was always talking about. How we decide that we're losers on Valentine's Day when crushes post pictures of the flowers that were sent to their office.

After the Tallahassee trip, I lost a few days to Mr. White Wine and I watched Korean soap operas on Hulu.com. I was trying to figure out how to ditch the resolution. I went on Facebook and noticed I was picking up friends. I sent messages, saying, "I'm only obligated to visit the original 325 friends, but if I am in your neighborhood..." And I got a lot of messages from people who had read the blog, seen the videos, noticed what I was doing—and they wanted to know that they thought it was cool. Or how could they stop being afraid of flying. Or of just meeting new people. I didn't know how to answer.

And some of my Facebook friends on my list were contacting me.

Answering messages from weeks before, saying, "I wondered when it was going to be my turn." Suggesting things to do. I had the first experience of someone saying, "This is what I want to do a video about." A friend hosted a party for me and several mutual Facebook friends. And while there were people who messaged, "That's the stupidest idea ever," there were others who messaged, "I wish I could do that."

Purpose was not yet ready to let go of me. And so I was propelled away from the Korean soap operas and had to rinse out my wineglass and put it in the dishwasher.

I had failed at so many things or not taken advantage of opportunities. I had never made a big mark in the world. I had started businesses and novels and gardens—and had failed because of something inside of me. An inability to get past blocks and obstacles because I tell myself in advance that I can't.

I decided that just this once, I would finish something without worrying about whether it was silly, strange, pathetic, or dumb.

I also gave into the notion that I might fail because of forces outside of my control. After all, to succeed, I had to have a perfect cooperation of 325 friends, the aviation industry, my car, Facebook, my finances. At the beginning of March, I had 265 friends to meet and 304 days in which to see them.

I decided to push failure off until tomorrow. And then the next day. And the next. Always telling myself that I could give up anytime I wanted.

I had two friends from Mexico City. One, Yoshi Maeshiro, was an actor who was part of the Facebook fan club for my grandfather Fritz. We had exchanged e-mails, and Yoshi expressed his admiration for Fritz's work. Enrique Celis from Mexico City? I had received a friendship request from him soon after I had become friends with Yoshi, and I assumed Enrique was a fan of Fritz. An uncommunicative friend, but a Facebook friend nonetheless.

Again, Reggie volunteered to be my chaperone for the trip. We would meet in Houston, fly into Mexico City late on Friday the eighteenth, and spend Saturday with Yoshi and Enrique. On Sunday morning, we'd fly back to Houston and part ways.

I marveled, and still do, at what loyalty and commitment Reggie brought to the venture. When I asked him why, he always said that he liked to travel and was just happy to go someplace without having the Army be in charge of his time. I also think of Reggie as my opposite—I think of a few blocks around my house as my world. He thinks of the entire world as his neighborhood.

There had been news reports of violence in the city, and the State Department had issued a warning advisory for travelers to Mexico in general. Reggie said we'd be okay if I followed his instructions: leave any jewelry at home, wear plain black clothes, and get a cheap backpack from Walmart. Leave the nice bag at home.

"I'm buying a pair of black sneakers from Payless," he messaged me a few days before we left. "I'm taking them out back of my house and smudging them up with mud."

I was surprised when we met in Houston's airport: Reggie is ordinarily a dapper man, but I walked right by the slim, nondescript black man in a black sweatshirt and jeans.

I wore a sweat suit so old and frayed that I was planning to throw it out at the end of the weekend.

We landed in Mexico City a little after ten that night. I should have been spooked by the silhouettes of men with automatic rifles on the rooftops of the downtown buildings. I should have been annoyed when the cab driver dropped us off at the wrong hotel, and we had to find another cab. Instead, I was tired and grateful to have made it this far.

Reggie took over the remote control and one of the beds. In the bathroom, I changed into a T-shirt and shorts. I took the bed next to the window and got out my computer.

"You should get some sleep," Reggie said.

"I'm tired, but I know I can't sleep."

"You should join the Army," Reggie suggested. "That'll teach you how to fall asleep anywhere, anytime."

And he went to sleep.

I logged on to Facebook. One confirmation message from Yoshi. He'd meet us at noon in the hotel lobby. But nothing from Enrique Celis. I messaged him again: a bright and cheerful note that I hoped didn't sound stalkerish. I replied to Yoshi.

> Me: So happy to see you! Will you have Enrique with you? Or maybe do you have a phone number for him?

I used my inhaler. I thought about how far away home was. How there was no way to get back to the safety of home. I watched the lights of the city go out and waited for the sun to come up. During the night, I opened up one of the bottled waters the hotel charged two dollars for. I noticed the seal had already been broken—someone had filled an empty. I thought why do we get told about things like tap water being dangerous? I drank the water.

Reggie woke up at six and said, "If you're not going to sleep, let's get going."

He had slept in his clothes, so we were on the street at six ten. I left the bag behind, only taking my passport, inhaler, and some cash. The hotel was in a strip of restaurants and hotels meant for tourists. Reggie had a map and a mission.

I wanted to see everything—thinking to myself I probably am never going to see Mexico City again.

We walked towards the train station. Three-sided tarp tents lined the sidewalk. Vendors in each tent sold candies, newspapers, and CDs. Some of the tents had generators. Christmas lights were strung up overhead, and counters in front of grills were manned by cooks gleaming with sweat. Commuters ate their breakfasts of chicken and rice. People were coming in from the trains and buses. Occasionally, we'd pass pairs of uniformed police carrying semi-automatic rifles.

"You look at things too long," Reggie said. "You stare. Never stare. Makes you look like a tourist. And give me your passport. It's sticking out of your fanny pack. You're going to get it stolen, and then we're going to have trouble. In fact, what are you doing with a fanny pack anyway?"

I ditched the pack.

We left the train station behind and came to the American Embassy in a quiet, nearly empty neighborhood. The building was squat, shuttered, fenced in with barbed wire. The guards were changing, and a couple of them stared at us.

"Now, lead us back to the hotel," Reggie said.

"I have no idea how to get back there."

"ArLynn, weren't you paying any attention?"

"Not particularly."

"Okay, here's the deal," Reggie said. He looked exactly like Joseph or Eastman about to launch into a lecture about how the world worked. Except in this case, I was prepared to listen because he knew what he was going to be right about it. "You are going to a lot of different places. You should always know where your embassy is in relation to where you are without using a map or a phone or asking for directions."

On the way back to the hotel, we stopped at every intersection, and I paid attention.

We waited for Yoshi in the lobby. I recited the fifteen twists and turns required to get to the embassy. Reggie smiled when I was done.

"Is it really that dangerous here?" I asked.

"Some parts, yes. I gotta tell you when I went to my commanding officer and said I wanted to come here, he didn't give me permission."

"Oh my God, are you going to be in trouble?"

He shrugged.

"Not if everything goes the way it's supposed to. And this trip, I want something."

"Whatever it is, it's yours."

"I want a great margarita out of the deal. If I'm going to be in Mexico City I want that margarita."

He looked over my shoulder.

"Is that your guy?"

I turned around on the bar stool.

"Yeah, how'd you know?"

"I went through his Facebook page. I wasn't coming down here without knowing who we were seeing."

Yoshi Maeshiro walked into the lobby and looked around. He was taller than I expected. His hair was longer than I had remembered from his picture. I walked up to him, and we started to shake hands before unconsciously agreeing on a friendly hug. There was a moment when we looked at each other that cemented months of messages and funny posts. He formally shook hands with me and Reggie. His English was a little worse than I expected—when you're writing, you have a chance to reflect and correct. But his English was way better than my Spanish, which was, sadly, zero.

"We have to find this guy a margarita," I told Yoshi.

"Ah, then I shall take you to the café where Che Guevera and Castro designed the revolution."

Yoshi guided us in the direction opposite to that of the train station and the embassy. He explained that he had come in on another train and that he lived outside the city proper. We passed a procession of Star Wars fans dressed in character. We saw ice cream vendors, crunk dancers, and policemen on horses at the Plaza de Revolution. We were swept up in a protest march against the government, but I had a difficult time understanding Yoshi's explanation of what people were protesting.

At the café, Reggie ordered a margarita. Yoshi picked out for us a variety of dishes that he said were the best.

He explained how the entertainment industry works in Mexico—he had trained in the academy for many years, as does every other actor. We talked about science fiction. We marveled at some of the Star Wars characters who drifted into the café to order drinks. Yoshi explained how the café was a great historical treasure for his country and for the revolution. Growing up, I had never heard nice things about Castro, and even though Che's picture was on t-shirts my sons had worn when they wanted to show their social justice cred, I had never understood why he was such a hero.

Now I was hearing history from a completely different perspective. From someone who believed passionately in the ideals of that revolution hatched in this café. And I decided I liked my friend. Yoshi was the kind of guy I would have lunch with if he lived nearby.

"By the way, I have been trying to find Enrique Celis," I said as the waiter took away our plates.

"To be honest, I do not even know who he is."

"But he's a mutual friend!"

"I think I might have gone to school with him. But I know nothing about who he is. He's just a friend on Facebook."

The sun was starting to slip down behind the mountains that ring the city. Reggie's margarita had been untouched since the first sip—he said it didn't taste like he expected. I had used my inhaler four times and was still having trouble breathing. Yoshi said that the smog is bad in the city because it rests on the valley of a volcano. He walked us back to the hotel. Saying good-bye was slightly awkward, because both of us knew that the odds of meeting again were fairly remote. Our friendship would continue on Facebook but not so much in real life.

I realized I had failed on two fronts: getting Reggie a great margarita and seeing Enrique Celis.

"Why don't you go out tonight on your own?" I suggested to Reggie. "You're in Mexico City. It's Saturday night. Go have fun."

"Can't. I'm beat. And besides, we have to get out of the hotel no later than six thirty if we're going to make our flight."

While he watched a Will Smith movie, I repacked my bag. I threw away every nonessential item, including receipts, magazines, T-shirts, and my sweat suit. In the shower, the water ran down my body and puddled black. Even though I usually can't sleep unless I have my earplugs, an eye mask, and a sedative, I fell asleep while Will Smith saved the world with a quick wit and far too many explosives.

Reggie woke me at four thirty.

"I can't go back to sleep," he said. "I'm going out for a bit."

"The business center is on the second floor," I said, thinking he was probably going to check his e-mail or his Facebook page. After all, it's what I would have done.

I woke up again at six thirty.

"Oh, jeez, Reggie, we're going to be..."

I rolled over. Reggie's bed was empty. I called his cell. He didn't pick up, and I left a message. I went downstairs to the business center and then the lobby and back upstairs. I left another message and started packing his things. I did the business center and lobby circuit again. I checked out of the room with his things. I called again. I stood outside on the sidewalk. I paced the lobby and called him again. He picked up.

"Hey, ArLynn."

He sounded pretty chipper.

"Where are you?"

"I'm at a salsa bar."

"We have a flight in two hours!"

"Chill."

He hung up. A half hour later, I saw him running from a block away. I put my hand up for a cab and was lucky. It was a Sunday morning. We flew on the highway, passing pastel houses and businesses with signs I couldn't understand.

"Did you get your margarita?"

"Yeah."

"Okay, now, what's going to happen if we don't make the plane?"

"We'll make the plane," he said and closed his eyes. I fidgeted in the seat, tried to get my seatbelt to work, pulled my phone out of my bag every few minutes to check on the time.

"Continental?" the cab driver asked as we entered the terminal drive.

"Continental," I said.

Reggie woke when we were dropped at the curb. When we reached the counter, the woman looked at us with a certain amount of impatience.

"Continental international flights are in the C terminal," she said.

"How do we get there?" Reggie asked as if he were merely satisfying a curiosity.

"The train," she said, and she looked over his shoulder at the next customer.

"We're in the wrong terminal?" I cried. Definitely a heart attack coming. Or maybe just anaphylactic shock. Or a stroke. Or maybe just a spontaneous combustion.

"You need to chill," Reggie said.

We found the train linking the four terminals and got in line for security. We now had twenty minutes to get on the plane. Reggie talked up two young women who were going to California. I fumed as a heated exchange broke out between a man at the front of the line and the security agents. The man was carrying a chicken in a small wooden box, and he must have lost the argument because after a few minutes, he and his chicken abandoned their efforts to get past security. He stomped past us and if I had understood a word of what he was shouting, I am sure my ears would have burned.

If I missed my flight, I had no idea how I was going to get to Houston and from Houston to Memphis and from Memphis back home.

If Reggie missed the flight, I couldn't imagine what kind of trouble he would be in.

"Reggie, how can you be so calm?"

"Because I've never missed a flight and I don't intend to start now. And getting nervous here isn't going to help matters."

We got to the gate as the line was forming for boarding. There was a second round of security by the American TSA. I was just starting to think about the fact that I had missed the preflight beer. I handed the ticket agent my passport and ticket. She shook her head.

"She's asking if you have your declaration form," Reggie said.

"Declaration?"

"That slip of paper the flight attendant gave you when we got here."

I thought back to the flight into Mexico. There had been a slip of paper that the flight attendant handed to me and to every other passenger.

"I threw it away. I was trying to get everything in my bag, so last night I threw everything away that I didn't need. I didn't know I needed that."

Reggie and the ticket agent both looked at me. I felt the crush of the impatient people behind us. The ticket agent called over her supervisor. He guided me away from the line and explained that I would have to go to the Immigration Desk.

"See ya," I said to Reggie, and I took off my shoes. I ran back through the terminal to the Immigration Desk, and as I waited in line, that's when I realized: I was in an airport. I was in another country. I was in a country where I didn't know the language. Where I made mistakes that other people found ludicrous.

And I was alone.

I reached the head of the line and explained my problem to the agent. My story apparently was something she had heard before because without a word, she handed me a sheet from a pad of forms. I recognized the word Declaration. I figured *nombre* was Spanish for *name*, but just about everything else was a mystery. I started to cry.

"Why did you throw it out?"

I couldn't believe Reggie had followed me, but he had. He filled out the form for me, and I returned to the Immigration Desk where it was duly stamped. Then we hustled back to the gate. I presented the form, but the bureaucratic verve had gone out of the ticket agent. Without looking at it, she tossed it on her desk. Reggie and I entered American security where agents gave us a once-over. We were the last passengers to get on the plane.

"Told you I wasn't going to miss a flight," Reggie boasted.

He found his seat. I was seated next to a toddler and his mom. I was drained and sweaty and needed a preflight beer or a tranquilizer. The toddler bounced in his seat as the plane pulled away from the gate.

I felt a fluttering in my chest. Was I going to be able to pull out of what was shaping up to be a full-blown anxiety attack? I looked at the toddler who seemed to think this was an amusement park ride. And then I made a choice. I would be excited. I would think like a toddler.

I can't say it made a lot of difference. But I didn't know what else to do. And then, as we rose up in the air, I thought about Enrique Celis. Odds were pretty good that I wouldn't be able to squeeze another trip to Mexico City into the itinerary. I couldn't afford it in time or in money. So in some sense, I had now officially declared myself a failure.

But I had gotten on a plane. I had visited Mexico City. I had gotten to know Yoshi so that when we messaged or commented on each other's pages, we knew the person at the other end of the Facebook connection. I had learned how another person could have a completely opposite view of how the world works and still we could be friends.

I also learned that whenever a flight attendant hands you a piece of paper, hang on to it.

We landed at Houston and Reggie ran for his connecting flight—with just ten minutes to find the Continental domestic flight terminal—and as he tossed a goodbye in my direction, I realized I was having fun.

# April—Friends 86-111: Unfriending (Part 1)

Every day, when you're a kid, you might meet your new best friend on the playground, at camp, in school. You go home on the camp bus, you graduate, your parents move. You hang on to some friends and some disappear.

When you get your first job, you feel really tight with your coworkers, but the time together doesn't necessarily extend to beyond nine-to-five confidences and the occasional drinks after hours. And when you leave the job, you say you'll keep in touch, it'll be just like before. But it isn't, and suddenly, you realize it's been five years since you've seen each other.

When you're a parent, the opportunities to meet your new best friend are even more limited: you find yourself friends with the parents of your children's friends, and well, what you've got in common is that you're the parents of your kids' friends.

In the dark ages before social networking, if you wanted to find the kid you were friends with in high school but whom you've lost touch with, the first step was to find the parents and ask them for an address. But if the parents had moved away, if nobody had kept up with them, pretty soon, the trail goes cold. Now, the first thing you do when you have a lonely hankering to find out what happened to your lab partner from chemistry class is Google their name. The second is to look them up on Facebook.

I had a lot of friends on my list who were "wow, what have you been doing for the last thirty years?" friends. In the few years I had been on Facebook, I had three times received Facebook friendship requests from gentleman callers from before I was married.

When I went through my list of friends at the beginning of the year, I noticed that none of these ex-boyfriends were my friends. I had been defriended or unfriended, which was as easy as a click—much easier than whatever breakup had occurred in the distant past. Facebook is so sensitive to the delicacies of ego that you are never informed that you are defriended, it just happens.

I had decided that some relationships deserved to remain in the past. But there were other relationships that I should have recognized were toxic reminders of the past—packed with resentments, anger, hostility, and ambiguity that couldn't be smoothed with three decades cooling off. One such encounter with the past occurred in April, and so Chaucer is right, it really was the cruelest month.

It didn't start that way. After the trip to Mexico City, I was full of confidence and keeping up with numbers and forgiving myself the notion that success was not going to strictly be a numbers game. I went to New York and realized that I'm not really friends with the science fiction novelist Glen Thater. He uses Facebook to promote his books, and I could e-mail him every day of the year and say, "how about coffee?" and the best I would get is a restraining order for stalking.

I wasn't really friends with Gilbert Gottfried, the comedian, although I did become his Facebook friend before his account became a fan page. While I was in New York, Mr. Gottfried twittered some offensive remarks about a devastating earthquake in Japan. I wasn't feeling too kindly towards him anyway for ignoring my messages and adding to my failure rate, and I held an online poll of my other Facebook friends. Overwhelmingly, the decision was defriend—so I did. I think Mr. Gottried was more saddened by losing his AFLAC commercial gig.

I met with friends in New York, came home for only a few days, and headed back out to Chapel Hill to meet two daughters of a college professor and faculty wife who had been as close to a surrogate family as could be. And then, I started on an ambitious (for me) weeklong road trip through the middle southeast of the country. I drove to Cincinnati, into West Virginia, through Pennsylvania to Delaware, and then back to Philadelphia and into central Pennsylvania.

I was born in 1960. I can remember when the reason for a woman to get a college degree was so that she could raise her children to be cultivated and intelligent. Sex before marriage? Completely wrong. Living together without being married? Well, the obvious answer is why should a man buy the cow when he can have the milk for free? I can remember when interracial marriage was scandalous, even if I wouldn't have known it was illegal in some states. Littering? We did it all the time. Smoking cigarettes? There were ashtrays at every restaurant table and even the library had a smoking lounge. Gays? Lesbians? Transgendered individuals? Not even something to be discussed.

By the time I was sixteen years old, I had been in several foster and group homes. I had lost ground in high school and had finally dropped out. I had an unexpected opportunity to go to a community college without getting a GED, and my high school friend George's family volunteered to take me in. The county social worker agreed, and I couldn't believe my good fortune. I would have a chance to get a good education, and I would get a job and live a great life. I was grateful beyond measure.

But there was a price.

George's father paid a lot of attention to me. He taught me how to play the guitar. He asked for my help when he built an addition onto the house. He valued my opinion and told me repeatedly that I was pretty and smart. Words every sixteen-year-old wants to hear.

The first time he kissed me, I was horrified—and he assured me that it would never happen again. The second time, he explained that it was my fault: I was irresistible. The third time when I protested, he explained again how it was my fault. And how I owed him.

The fourth time, how if I didn't cooperate, he could get the county to take me away.

I'd get in trouble with the law. I'd never finish college.

It's tough to believe, but it made sense to me. I had a secret I had to keep. A horrific one.

And it made sense to George that telling his parents his own secret wasn't a good idea. But that he could tell me.

One weekend, I came back to what I thought was an empty home to find George sitting in the kitchen wearing his mother's pearls, cocktail dress, and wig. I was completely baffled.

And a little horrified because the wig was not a good look.

"I just feel more comfortable in women's clothes," he explained.

I tried to be as supportive as possible, even going so far as to shop for clothing with him. All while plotting how to get out of the home. A few months after I managed that, George left for college.

We lost touch until he contacted me on Facebook. As Georgeanne.

She messaged that she was on permanent full disability because her car trunk lid had fallen on the back of her neck when she was unloading documents for an employer. Unfortunately, the Social Security Administration wouldn't pay for the operation to change her body to reflect her gender. Instead, she took a mix of hormones to allow her to maneuver through her public life as a woman. She worked on an online interactive comic series that she hoped would one day be a paying gig.

A few cautious "what have you been up to" messages later, Georgeanne finally asked, "Did you ever sleep with my father?"

I was prepared for that.

I didn't lie. I told her yes, but that it wasn't consensual. She said she had always known. Georgeanne had little contact with his family because they couldn't accept her as a woman who lived with a woman who had also been born a man.

I warned Georgeanne that I blogged about every Facebook friend I visited. I invited her to look at the blog and see if she had any limits about what I was writing. I gave every friend that opportunity, and sometimes after a visit, someone would say that one thing or another should be changed or deleted or clarified. It didn't bother me. Sometimes, people wanted to reveal more than I thought they should. But I was particularly cautious about Georgeanne.

Georgeanne said that she didn't care what I wrote.

I was surprised but admired that position.

I parked in the driveway of a two-story saltbox house in central Pennsylvania, on a Tuesday evening. I was met by Georgeanne and her partner Marie.

"Do you mind if we use our car?" Georgeanne asked. "It's a little roomier."

"That's fine. Where do you want to go?"

There was a Chinese restaurant in town that they favored. I couldn't see any difference between George and Georgeanne except possibly that Georgeanne's hair was longer. Marie and Georgeanne looked like two middle-aged lesbians. In a college town, they'd be the couple that organized the food co-op and the poetry slam night.

Georgeanne had suffered mightily with her gender at college both internally and because of bullying, taunting, and worse. After we ordered appetizers, she told me about being raped by a professor at her college and how she suppressed the memory for years.

It's one thing to read about someone's misery and another to sit across the table as it is retold. I was horrified on her behalf.

Against her better judgment, she had married a woman and became a father. She was talented enough that she felt she could express herself as a woman more at her office than she could at home. At one point, her boss told her to just be done with it, to come out as a woman because the ambiguity was confusing to others her coworkers.

George went home on a Friday afternoon and explained to her wife that from that weekend on, she would be Georgeanne.

Georgeanne would have been happy to continue being married but his wife was uninterested. Once divorced, Georgeanne didn't get to see their daughter for years. And now, as an adult, Georgeanne had no contact with her daughter except through Facebook. Marie's daughter had reached out to her and was trying to persuade her that family is family, and it's okay to have a father who is now another mother.

Georgeanne wanted more than anything to finish the gender change. She had fought with the employer over disability payments and then with insurance companies and the Social Security Administration. The saving grace of her life was meeting Marie on a transgender-friendly computer networking site that was a precursor to the Internet.

I would be lying if I said I felt close to Georgeanne as I settled up the check and we headed for the parking lot. I hope that I am not fooling myself into thinking that

I am free of bigotry against people who begin life with one gender and switch to another. I was frankly relieved as we returned to their house to drop them off. I was looking forward to the hotel. I had been on the road for seven days and needed a good sleep before what would be a fifteen-hour drive back to Chicago. I was already thinking about where I would eat breakfast and whether I would take the turnpike or aim for the slightly longer but way less aggravating state highway. I was in the back seat, and it was easy to close my eyes for a moment.

"Oh, yeah, Dad was a real bastard," Georgeanne said.

She had brought me up-to-date on his parents. Father had died of emphysema. Mom was devoted to him until the end and maintained a steady belief that they would be reunited in heaven. Georgeanne only knew of this through her sister, who was her friend on Facebook, if not in real life.

"Yeah, you weren't the only foster sister he was banging," Georgeanne said as the car pulled into their driveway. "But I'll never forget the way I found out. I came to your dorm room, and you answered the door naked, waving a champagne bottle. You thought I was going to be Dad."

I had an unbelievable urge to kick the back of her seat. Hard. What she said was wrong. On so many different levels. I had extricated myself from the home precisely so I could get away from his Dad. I wouldn't open a door naked. And where would I have gotten champagne?

Marie concentrated on pulling the car into the parking space as if she had never before tried such a difficult maneuver. Without a word, we got out of the car. Georgeanne and I squared off. Georgeanne lifted her chin—the lens of her glasses reflected the streetlights. And her entire demeanor spoke this way: "I might hate my dad and my ex-wife and a host of other people who have done me wrong, but just remember you don't get away without feeling some of my hate. And you will never be anything more than a sixteen-year-old my dad was banging. Just remember that."

Marie came around to the passenger side of the car.

"It was so nice meeting you," she said. "I hope we can do this again sometime."

I sucked in a harsh breath.

"Yeah, it really was a lot of fun," I said.

We exchanged hugs. Marie and me. Georgeanne and me. I got in my car as Marie and Georgeanne went into the house.

I pulled out of the driveway.

I was furious. I was trembling. I missed the turn for my hotel. I was crying as I walked through the lobby. I cried for most of the night.

And the next morning, I drove home. I listened to talk radio, music, a recorded book. I stopped at a Starbucks in Ohio and posted a blog that was so chipper and sugary that it sounded like Santa Claus and the Tooth Fairy had been the previous evening's dinner table companions. I was careful about my explanation for our friendship—everyone we went to high school with knew Georgeanne had been George.

I devised a truncated explanation that said, "I met Georgeanne, whom I knew from the past as George, in high school."

Then I sent Georgeanne the link and wrote that if there was anything she wanted changed, she should get back to me as soon as possible and I would take it down.

I hit Like on her latest link to the comic series she wrote. I'm not saying I read it, but I was propelled by a weird mix of thirty five year old guilt and twelve hour old anger.

Coming into Winnetka, I drove to the grocery store and bought two bottles of white wine.

I was sixteen again, and I knew it was wrong. I knew that it wasn't the first time Georgeanne's father had done this. Even then, I figured it wasn't going to be the last. I didn't have the courage to say no, and frankly, he had played it well: using all my attention-starved weaknesses against me. And when I understood what a horrific trade I had made for it, I still didn't get out for a full year and a half. I didn't rat him out, not because I was so concerned about preserving his family, but because I was terrified of all the trouble I might be in.

I was fifty years old, and there was a permanent black mark in my soul that I had been carrying for thirty-four years. And I had reopened every poorly sutured wound on Facebook.

I would never say anything to her, but I wasn't going to forgive Georgeanne for her comment.

I wasn't going to forgive her father, even if he was dead.

And I wasn't ever going to forgive myself.

# May—Friends 111 through 141: Basic Info: Religious Beliefs

I had Facebook friends from college I hadn't seen in the thirty years since graduation. John Finnegan who had been in theater and whom I had stood up on a date for Valentine's Day (he forgave me). There was Tim Crawford, a football player turned navy seaman who took me out for a pedicure when I explained my project. Navy vets are tough because when the technician put our feet in hot wax, I cried and Tim was just cool with it. There was Bruce Nesmith, who now taught at Cole College and posted links to opinion pieces he wrote for newspapers.

But the first Facebook friend I knew from North Central College was Mike Coglan. Facebook suggests friends, and early in 2008, Facebook thought that we should be friends. After all, we went to the same college thirty years before. I remembered Mike as being one of those cool kids. I know we took economics together. He was compact, athletic, cheerful. We started exchanging messages. He beat me at Scrabble. Many times over.

Mike had meant to go on the trajectory of business school, moneymaking, prestige. Instead, he married, joined the ministry, and was assigned a small congregation in Kearney, Missouri. He was happy, content, only occasionally doubtful of his relationship with God. I became friends with his wife Laura. I read his weekly sermons that he e-mailed to congregants who weren't able to make services.

I was writing a history of Winnetka for Arcadia Publishing Company. It is a money-losing proposition to write books for Arcadia, but I wanted to do one for the town in which I lived, the town my boys had called their home. When the recession hit, Mike wrote that his congregation had been hit really hard. I suggested I come to Kearney and write a history of the town with him. With Charlie agreeing to take care of the images, I was confident we could gather the materials and have a first draft done in a month. And Mike could use the author discount to purchase copies and then devise some sort of fundraiser for the church in which the copies would be resold at full price.

Charlie and I drove to Kearney. The first order of business was speaking at the local Rotary Club where I asked for help from the members—photographs, memories, contacts, anything. Charlie sat in the back of the room with Mike.

"What do you remember about ArLynn from when you guys went to college together?"

"I don't remember her at all," Mike admitted.

The book was written over the course of several months, although Charlie and I were there for only a weekend scanning people's family albums, visiting graveyards and family farms, and going to Mike's Sunday service.

In May 2011, I planned a road trip through Iowa, crossing over into Nebraska, and coming down into Missouri. I took tornadoes with me. In Cedar Rapids, in Council Bluffs, in Blue Springs, and again in Kearney as I drove into town. I spent the first hour in town in the beer locker at Kearney's one bar.

I had eight friends in Kearney. And I hadn't seen any of them since working on the book. Darryl the hairdresser (and president of the historical society) cut my hair and explained how he was using Facebook to promote his business beyond the town's borders.

"I'm selling products through Facebook," he explained. "And so I picked the name Haircut Salons and I advertise all sorts of Kearney businesses."

I had dinner with the waitress from the Italian restaurant where Charlie and I had eaten every night during our last stay. I went to city hall and found out my Facebook friend the mayor had left a message for me saying that his cancer treatments were leaving him too weak to see me. I left him a message saying I hoped he recovered soon. I wasn't taking Facebook failures too seriously.

On the last night, the Coglans hosted a dinner for several of my Facebook friends. The next morning, I got a call from Mike.

"Laura wants you to come over to the house for breakfast. She wants to talk to you."

I don't know about you, but when I hear "we have to talk" or "somebody wants to talk to you," I get a funny, horrible, gravity pull on my stomach. Had I done something to offend her? Had I said something wrong? Was she mad because I had spent the tornado in the beer locker? I came to the Coglan home prepared for a lecture, a breach, a falling out. I made a quick check on my Facebook account. Laura had not defriended me so that either meant that whatever was wrong wasn't that big of a deal or. . . , that she wasn't as compulsive as I was about Facebook.

We got our coffee and pastries and took them out to the living room. Laura is a beautiful, quiet, elegant woman, and she quite obviously had something on her mind.

"I've been reading your blog," she said. "And it hurts me."

Oh, no, the post about how much fun it was to hang out in the beer locker!

"You think that God doesn't love you."

Nope. It was the post I had written after coming back from Pennsylvania. About Georgeanne. Well, actually not about Georgeanne, but about me and her father. I had been very honest, maybe too honest, about my relationship with him and the guilt I carried with me. And the white wine and Korean soap opera bender that followed.

"Think about your own sons."

Joseph and Eastman. I knew they didn't read my blog. They loved me, to be sure, but not enough to be particularly curious. That's the nature of boys who become men who have lives way more interesting than that of their parents.

"I wouldn't have too much of a problem with them knowing about...well, you know...because they know I grew up in different foster homes and stuff."

"I'm not talking about that," she said with surprising firmness. "I'm talking about what would *you* feel like if you knew that they thought you didn't love them."

"Oh, Laura, of course I love them and I tell them every day. They're probably sick of hearing me say it, and oh, jeez."

"Yeah, that's how God must feel."

My eyes were filling up. If I blinked, tears would drop down on my cheek. So I opened my eyes as wide as I could.

"God wants you to feel that love," she said firmly. "Just the same as you want Joseph and Eastman to know that you love them."

"I've done a lot of awful things. Even aside from thirty four years ago."

"Whatever you've done."

The cool air had dried my eyes so I could blink.

My religious beliefs are strange and somewhat contradictory—which I'm sure is true for a lot of people. I can't give up a belief that God exists, that Jesus was born, that Jesus died and rose. I am a mishmash of Protestant and Catholic details. But I had a firm belief that I was outside of the saved, the elect, the loved. That I was going to end up in Hell.

Many Facebook friends shared their spiritual traditions over the course of the year.

"Try to imagine, just even for a second, what you'd feel like if you believed God loves you. That's the peace he wants for you."

I did, for just a second. And it didn't give me peace. It gave me more of those tears so that now all I needed was a red Afro wig, and I'd be cast in a traveling production of *Little Orphan Annie*.

The most sacred and important moments of our lives are often in the most mundane places and without the accompaniment of soaring Hayden music and incense. Instead, I was in a nicely furnished Kearney Missouri home. Aware of how my coffee cup was cold. That I had to pee. That I was supposed to meet my last Facebook friend of Kearney in twenty minutes. And that a neighborhood dog would not stop barking. And that I had been with a number of other Facebook friends who shared their faiths and their traditions. I had meditated, possed, sweated, and attended services in a dozen different faiths.

But I have never to this day felt as powerfully moved as I was in the Coglan home.

"Well, that's what I had to say to you," Laura said.

And I wanted to sit on her lap and keep crying.

I went back to being me. Just me. She stood up. I stood up. We hugged. I wasn't sure about God at that moment, but I was sure about Laura. She loved me even if I wasn't the best candidate for anybody's love. I pulled away and started laughing. Which is what I do when I want to get out of emotionally tough situations.

"I'm going to pour myself another cup of coffee," Mike said, clapping his hands together. "Want some?"

"Just half a cup," I said. "I gotta be at the firehouse. I'm Facebook friends with the Chief. He wants to swear me in as a volunteer fireman. Firewoman."

"When are you going to see Ian?" Laura asked, deftly moving the conversation away from the intense.

Their son Ian was also my Facebook friend, and as a missionary, he had been sent to Nome, Alaska.

"I've got one other friend in Homer, on the southern tip of the state. I'm aiming for September."

On the drive back to Chicago, I tried imagining the sensation of spiritual peace. Like what I would feel like if I didn't fear death and eternal judgment, if I believed in God's love, if I were secure. I couldn't do it for more than ten seconds at a time without crying.

I got pulled over by a state trooper just before reaching the Illinois border. I knew exactly what I could do to get the tears going, but I didn't. I employed a different strategy.

"Does it help that I'm a volunteer fire officer for Kearney?" I asked.

The trooper was supremely unimpressed and gave me a ticket. One hundred and fifty smackers.

I began to pray from that visit on. Every day working to imagine what I would feel like if I believed in a God who loved me.

And maybe, in a weird way, I owe that to my Facebook friend Georgeanne as much as to the Coglans.

# June—Friends 142 through 166: Likes

In late May, I messaged Winfield. I had met him five years before in a downtown bar—he had been reading a comic book and drinking a Malbec, which is an unusual conversation starter combination of naïf and sophistication. Every six months or so, he would invite me to a party, to Fourth of July fireworks, to a ball game. In between, I wouldn't hear from him, and at one point, he moved to Nevada and then came back to the North Shore.

> Me: When can I take you to a Cubs game?
>
> Winfield: You only want to see me for your stupid Facebook project! I have tried to date you for years, and you haven't given me the time of day! Forget it!

I considered the prospect of me and Winfield in a romantic entanglement. It might be nice, but now, it looked like the window of opportunity had passed. And thus, Winfield was added to the list of friend failures.

It was June when I started to worry about money. And money, or the lack of it, was just another way of failing. One that would be a quiet failure.

People asked me how I paid for this adventure. I was always surprised because I was brought up to believe that asking any question along those lines—how much did you pay for your house? How much do you get paid? What did those shoes cost?—was vulgar. But people asked.

My son Joseph was a film major and my younger son Eastman a drummer. As soon as I figured out that neither had a fallback career in mind, I started saving money. I offered Joseph seed money to make his first film when he graduated. I offered him thirty thousand dollars.

"Are you going to want to be part of it?" he had asked me.

"You mean, help out? Produce? Write? Sure."

"Then, no, I don't want your money."

It stung at first, but he had a point. I'm too much of a "here's my idea!" sort of person. It would be impossible for me not to want to be involved, to make suggestions, to pout when those suggestions weren't taken seriously, and it would be impossible for him to be a man and not a mama's boy.

So I started the year with thirty thousand dollars in the bank that was mine to gamble with. By June, I was running on empty. Plane tickets, hotel rooms, dinners, lunches, gas, new tires for a very tired car. I used Kayak, Orbitz, Priceline, and asked for frequent flyer miles from anybody who could spare them.

I had priced out international tickets, and the best I could do was seven thousand for an around the world ticket that would take me to South Korea, Taiwan, the Philippines, India, United Arab Emirates, Turkey, Italy, Germany, England, and back home in a dizzying seventeen days. If I included a chaperone and sleeping at hotels not more expensive than park benches, I probably couldn't do it.

And then, I went to dinner at Facebook friends Ben and Marissa's home. The dinner set in motion the worst turn of events—all because of the most fundamental flaw in my character: vanity.

The dinner was proposed by Marissa, a stay-at-home mom who loved her son Desmond and loved spending time with him but was reeling from having recently been part of a mass firing at her graphics design firm. I had originally met her husband Ben when he worked at Strata entertainment on a family my son Eastman was in—but also, I knew Ben because of his uncle Lawrence.

Lawrence was a best-selling author and a photographer who lived on the North Shore. Years before, when I was forty-seven and feeling the pull of age after separating from Stephen, Lawrence persuaded me to pose for a series of nude photographs. He said he was devising a coffee table book of middle-aged women—and he showed me a series of photographs he had already done. They were nothing one wouldn't see in *Vogue* or *Bazaar* magazine if either magazine decided to use middle-aged models to promote accessories or to make the three times a year "accept your body" editorial counterpoint to all the young, anorexic supermodels they use every other issue. I wasn't to be the obese woman, the mastectomy survivor, or even the Caesarian gal. I was apparently to be the reasonably average forty-seven-year-old. I did the shoot with three glasses of white wine in me, and I was not unhappy with the results.

When I first met Ben, it was because Eastman would be in a film Ben was working on, and Ben said, "I recognize you. Your backside is on my uncle's mantle."

Dinner was a quiet June evening. Ben and Marissa lived in a three-story flat on the north side of the city, and I brought flowers as a hostess's gift. We went out to the backyard. Their son Desmond wore just a diaper and played with children from the neighborhood.

Marissa and I talked about our respective Facebook friends. Posts we had seen. Marissa fretted that I wasn't to do a video unless she had done her hair and makeup. She asked Ben to watch Desmond while she prepared.

"What are you talking about, doing a video?" Ben asked.

"Oh, she can explain it," Marissa said and went into the house.

He looked at me. Ben was thirtysomething, sported what he proudly described as a Jew-fro, and every few moments, he pushed his glasses back up his nose in an oddly endearing gesture. He was funny and talked in staccato bursts. He was erudite in politics, music, film, philosophy, everything. I genuinely liked him. *This was exactly why I should meet my Facebook friends*, I thought.

I explained the New Year's resolution, and I had a bit of a defeatist tone. I was numerically making progress, I was reconnecting in a personal way with people I hadn't seen or didn't see very often. I was certainly getting out of the house. But I was feeling a bit like I was on a brakeless bicycle, heading downhill into a busy intersection. And I had no helmet.

"Do you understand how important your project is?" Ben asked. "I mean, that's like really universal. Facebook is everything right now. You're a genius! You're totally at the front end of our culture."

*Tell me more about how wonderful I am, Ben, because I am starting to fall apart a little on that point otherwise.* Instead, I said, "It helps me get out of the house."

"What do you mean?"

"I get anxiety attacks when I leave my house. I am awful. It's a big contributor to why I got divorced. Imagine a wife who won't go to dinner parties with you, won't leave the house at all for periods of time, and you know, there were other things. But it got to him."

"You have to meet Harry."

He went to retrieve a redhead gal who had several times made a track between Ben and Marissa's building and the one next door.

I might have given the appearance of dismissing his enthusiastic response, but I was feeling quite the opposite. Someone calls you a genius? It feels great. I really want to believe that I'm brilliant, beautiful, charming, and destined for great things.

Even if in reality, I was a fifty-year-old slightly overweight woman who'd raised her kids, recently became divorced, and was completely superfluous to the world.

But Ben said I was a genius.

Oddly, that made me think Ben must be a genius.

He brought over the redhead, who on closer inspection was a frazzled fiftyish replica of me. Ben excused himself to get another beer, said he'd bring me another, and asked Harry if she wanted one too. She declined.

"Ben told me about your project. I could never do it. I have far too many Facebook friends. I have more than a thousand."

"Wow," I said neutrally. Almost every person I had met during the course of the year told me their tally. If it was less than fifty, they claimed they were concerned about their privacy and suggested the obvious, which is that I could hardly know all my Facebook friends well. If it was more than five hundred, there was a certain braggadocio.

"I have a political blog for *Huffington Post*," Harry continued. "I'm heavily involved in social activism."

I knew enough to not comment.

"I have a really active social life online," she said. "But it's rough right now."

"Why don't you sit down?"

"No, that's okay. I'm doing laundry for my two sons. They're moving out this weekend, and I'm trying to help. The washing machine in my building is out, so I'm using Ben and Marissa's."

In fidgety starts and stops, she described her life: a job she had lost just a month before. How she had been able to leave the block because of her commute, but now, she couldn't manage to get off the block. The building, bought with her sons during boom times, was in foreclosure, and she and her sons agreed it was best for them to abandon the building. They were moving out the upcoming weekend. She wasn't sure how she would get to the grocery store, to the bank, to the drugstore. And what would she do when the bank took the house?

I saw myself in her. When Ben came back with a couple of beers, he insisted that she sit down, which made her bolt. She returned again when another load needed to be shifted from washer to dryer. With Ben around, she was less vulnerable and exposed. They discussed an ongoing Chicago political scandal. She knew everything and everybody—she was a player, and it might have only been online, but it meant something to her.

"Do you realize how much she wishes she were like you?" Ben asked when she was out of earshot. "You're like doing what people should be doing. Getting out from the computer. And also, you're tackling an issue of modern society. Anxiety disorder is totally a first world problem, and we have these ways of achieving a false intimacy when we don't even have to leave the privacy of our own homes."

He wasn't saying anything I hadn't wondered about. But the way he was saying it, with such excitement and punctuating his words with a push to his glasses, that made him seem so brilliant. I was entranced.

Marissa returned. She was a gorgeous woman, but with a little lipstick and mascara, she was a magazine cover girl. Ben started to tell her about what a genius I was. And as vain as I am, I felt like the kid with an unlimited credit at the ice cream store who finally says, "Enough." I asked them about how they met, which is a question that always gets a couple started and allows both to participate.

I drove home, and my chest was full of something I had been missing for a while—it might be called confidence, but I am not sure that it was exactly that. If Ben's flattery was as substantial as feathers, it was still a very firm pillow.

The next morning, I checked my Facebook page, and there was a message from Ben. It implored me to never give up the project, that it was important. So important that he thought it should be the subject of a documentary. And that he was ready to give up his job at Strata entertainment to do it.

I felt a momentary surge of panic as I messaged him.

> Me: I don't have any money to make a movie. And I don't want to be responsible for someone quitting their job.
>
> Ben: I want to do this. It's important. And I'm not asking you for money. That's what I do for Strata. I raise money to make movies. Just tell me I can make some phone calls about this.
>
> Me: Of course. But don't quit your job.
>
> Ben: If this works out the way I think it will, you won't have to pay another dime for travel expenses. But we have to move quickly. You're halfway through the year. This should have been happening in January.
>
> Me: Okay, but don't quit your job.

That evening, Ben called me. There were people interested. Investors. People with serious money. A guy in New York who put money into every movie Ben had been part of. A lady in Hawaii who suffered from agoraphobia and who could probably finance the entire budget.

"What is your budget?" I asked.

"I think it's come in around three hundred thousand dollars," Ben said. "But remember, it's not your money. In fact, the point is that you wouldn't have to pay for any expenses from here on out. My boss would like to invest in this, but he's got other projects he's doing."

"Wait. You talked to your boss? You didn't quit, did you?"

"No, of course not. Just that I told him what I'm doing."

"What *are* you doing?"

"I'm making a documentary about you. About your project. I believe in you and believe in what you're doing. And I'm willing to risk everything on this."

"Have you talked to Marissa about this?"

"Oh, yeah, totally! She understands that I've been unhappy in my job and that I was going to quit anyway. She's completely behind me on this one."

"Wait! Are you saying you *did* quit your job?"

"I've given them my two week notice. They're happy for me. They see the genius in this project."

"Ben, I don't have any money."

"I don't need your money. I'm going to be raising money."

"You're going to be able to raise money?"

"ArLynn," he said, stretching my name into a definite statement. "This is what I *do*. I raise money. That's what I do every day for a living."

"Okay."

"But I need to get started on this now. I need a prospectus for investors. I need to put together an agreement protecting both of us. I need to hire a crew. I need a publicity packet. I have to buy a camera. And I know the kind that would be perfect for this."

"This sounds like a lot."

"I have always wanted to do this, ArLynn, I just have never found the right subject. And I'm about to turn thirty-six. I have a son. I don't ever want to tell my son that I didn't at least try to follow my dream."

"So what do you need me to do?"

"Nothing. You don't to change anything you're already doing. Go on your trips. Meet your friends. Write your blog. And understand that the best birthday present you could ever give me is to say yes."

"Okay."

"Good enough."

The next morning I flew to Los Angeles. I put the matter of Ben out of my head. I met with Facebook friends and figured out that anybody who says they live in Los Angeles lives three hours away from anybody else who says they live in Los Angeles. And everybody in Los Angeles is in the film industry or believes they are in the film industry.

"This would make a good movie," I would sometimes hear.

And by feathery light increments, my chest filled. I was on to something. I wasn't a complete idiot. I got Facebook messages from Ben chronicling his progress: a college buddy agreeing to be assistant producer, a camera with a boom mike that was absolutely the best, contacts that he had made with people inside Facebook.

I came home feeling like maybe I was working on something important and not freakishly stupid. When my realtor said that after six months of being on the market, the house price had to be dropped again, I wasn't too concerned. After all, I was part of a film project now.

I got a phone call from Ben in late June.

"I'm not sure about things," he said. His voice wasn't the tippet tap-tap of excitement. Instead, he sounded as if he were struggling to form words at all. "I've got investors who want to put down money, but of course, their attorneys want to see a prospectus and a pre-trailer. And I can't find any way of financing those things. It's such a small thing, and everybody is ready to jump, just I can't get past this hurdle."

I swallowed. Hard.

"I'm not asking you for money. I'm just letting off steam."

There was a long, slowly spiraling silence.

"It's such a genius project," Ben said. "You know you could change lives. Someone like Harry. You could be an inspiration. You could change her life. You could change a lot of people's lives."

My chest nearly burst.

"How much do you need?" I asked at last.

# July—Friends 167 through 186: Defriending (Part 2)

"It's just paper money," Stephen said when I came to him. "It doesn't really exist. And if this is important to you, then do it. When the house sells, we deduct the money from your share of the proceeds."

"What if the house doesn't sell?"

"It's going to sell. The market has hit bottom, and it's going to turn around. Pretty soon, you're going to be rolling in money. So if you think he can make a movie and he needs some help to get started, feel free."

We took the money from the line of credit on the house. It only existed on paper, right? If the market picked up, the house would sell, and this was an investment, wasn't it? And if the market didn't pick up...I decided to not think about that.

And then Ben was everywhere. In the dining room with his laptop and his smartphone talking to people he said were excited about investing as soon as he put together a pre-trailer. On the front porch, smoking cigarettes with a crew—a producer, an assistant, a cameraman. He had a camera and lights, and he needed all of the extension cords that I kept in the attic with the Christmas ornaments. With my credit card, he booked the next two trips: New England and Southern California for me, himself, and his assistant Brandon—a laconic film student from Ohio.

"Wait, what happened to the money I loaned you?"

"I had to use that for lawyers to draw up a private placement agreement. And the camera. I priced it out, and it's cheaper to buy than to rent this equipment."

"I thought you were paying for your own tickets."

"Just until the money comes in, and then I'll repay you."

"Are you going to be able to raise this money?"

"ArLynn, that's what I *did* for my entire career."

Whenever we were out in public and he held the camera, people stared. There was a possibility that I was somebody they knew, that I was a celebrity, possibly an elderly Kardashian aunt.

I started to think I was funnier, smarter, more beautiful than before. That I had something important to say about Facebook, friendship, anxiety, our civilization, the universe.

The trips were shaped by Ben and Brandon's presence. Some people didn't like it and asked that they not be filmed. Ben would try to talk them out of it. I would feel stuck in the middle, between friendship and this project, which was now more crowded.

There were other friends who played for the camera, and I knew I was a peripheral person to the moment, that I wasn't necessary, and if I could just slip away, I could maybe get some peace.

And I was spending three times as much on travel expenses. And it wasn't worth asking him if he had raised any money because his answer was always the same dismissive "I *did* this for a living."

He wanted a list of my friends who had money. He was surly to me and Brandon. And when I said I didn't like that, he apologized.

"The problem is that I'm on the phone all day with investors, and you have to talk down to them," he said. "And then I forget that I need to tone it down when I get off the phone."

Things came to a head when we were in San Diego at the end of the month.

"I am absolutely devoted to this project," he said one evening when the three of us were having dinner. "But if I don't have an injection of cash, I am going to have to shut this down."

"What about your trailer?"

"I posted it on YouTube yesterday."

The trailer opened with a close-up of Ben. He was seated in his backyard on a lawn chair. He was sweating profusely. I could make out Harry's foreclosured building behind him.

"Hello, I'm Ben, and I'm here on the set of my latest film."

I clicked off.

"What? You didn't like it?"

"I'll look at it later."

I started to cry even before I got back to my hotel room.

I was vain. And even as I write this, I'm a vain old woman. I want to believe that I'm pretty, that I'm smart, that I'm charming, that I'm witty and funny, intelligent, friendly, beloved, everything. And I'm not. At least, not all the things at the same time. And not in the amounts I would like.

It was Ben's face, Ben's pronouncement that he was on the set of a latest film as if there was an entire oeuvre that was the subject of many film studies classes, Ben's lawn chair and the unpressed shirt, that made me see what this was worth. Yet I was his only investor. I was paying his bills. I wondered if it was time to cut my losses.

I didn't sleep well that night. Ripping my own skin off to reveal bloody pulp wouldn't have been any worse.

But my own vanity wasn't done with me.

The next evening, I was supposed to meet Facebook friend Alex. We had played Scrabble on Facebook for three years. He was in his midthirties, listed his professions as botanist and tax accountant, posted pictures of his weekends surfing and boating.

We had flirted online. I had often reminded him I was too old for him, and he dutifully said he had seen all my photos and I wasn't. A year before, he had been on a business trip in Chicago and we made arrangements to meet for dinner, but at the last minute, he had canceled.

I woke early and planned to find a toy shop. I wanted a Scrabble board. I figured dinner and maybe a coffee shop afterwards where we could play a game together. I would leave Ben and Brandon behind.

I got an early morning text:

> Alex: just got out of the doc's office. walking pneumonia. can't go out 2nite.
>
> Me: so sorry. get better soon.
>
> Alex: maybe u come over?
>
> Me: is that wise?
>
> Alex: want 2 give you hug be4 i go home. hotel lobby in 10?

I walked outside only to find Ben and Brandon waiting for me. I felt like a kid caught doing something wrong.

"What's up?" Ben asked.

"I'm going to the lobby. I'm not having dinner with Alex tonight. He's got pneumonia. He's just stopping by to say hi."

"This I gotta see."

"No, please, don't."

The Town and Country resort in San Diego is a complex of villas, a high-rise, and two-story motels abutting the parking lot. I walked across the gardens to the main building and stood outside. Ben stood beside me.

"Go away."

"This is my job. To record everything."

"He doesn't know you exist."

"I'll get a release from him."

"Just stop!" I snapped.

We stared at each other. He looked away first.

"If he stays for more than a minute, I'm coming out and filming him."

I waited by myself on the steps. A green pickup came into the parking lot and Alex got out. I recognized the Afro from his photos. He was shorter than I expected. He wore shorts and a T-shirt. He smiled when he saw me. We hugged.

"So what kind of drugs did they put you on?"

"You know, the usual."

"It's good to actually meet you."

He looked over my shoulder.

"Who's that?"

"Oh, I should have told you. He's a guy who's doing a documentary about this."

"I don't want to be on film."

"I gotta go. My doctor's appointment is in twenty minutes," Alex said.

"It was good to see you. Get better."

He got into his pickup and pulled out of the parking lot. I checked the texts. It didn't make sense. He had already gone to the doctor and gotten a diagnosis. And now he was saying he had to go to the doctor. I walked back to my room, trailed by Ben and Brandon. I was hardly listening to Ben's tirade about how I was interfering with his craft.

My phone vibrated.

> Alex: u r sexy

"What is it? What is it?" Ben asked.

> Alex: if i feel better 2nite u come nurse me?

"He wants me to come over."

"You're not going there by yourself."

"You're not the boss of me. If I go, I'm not going with you. You've scared him enough."

"But you're not going by yourself."

"I need some time on my own right now."

"That's exactly what I should be filming. But I have passes for Comic-Con, and I want to talk to some people, find out if I can make any contacts."

Me: text me if u feel better.

And then much later:

Alex: when u coming over?

Me: let's go out.

Alex: too sick.

Me: then i shldn't come over

I blogged about missing the chance to see Alex and I got to bed early. The next day, we flew back to Chicago. It was 2:00 a.m. of my birthday. The rain was so heavy the airport was shut down soon after our flight landed. The cab driver dropped me off at the house. Stephen had been staying at the house in my absence, and he came out to the curb with an umbrella. The lawn was flooded.

"How bad inside?" I asked.

"Take a look for yourself."

I went to the basement door. Opened it. The water was halfway up the stairs. Stephen brought me a glass of champagne.

"Happy birthday," he said.

We toasted and sipped and I closed the basement door.

"What do we do if the house doesn't sell?"

"Even if we drop the price another fifty, you'll still clear some money," Stephen said. "And I still think the market has just bottomed out. You'll have some money to get a new place."

"Except for the Ben money."

"Yeah, but isn't his film going to make you money?"

And what I thought was *No, that money is gone and will never be seen again.*

Two months later, I was in Montreal and checked my phone when I woke up. Alex. He had called four times overnight. I wondered if it was a drunk dial or a butt dial. We had played a Scrabble game just the day before.

I listened to the voice mail.

"You wrote about meeting me," Alex said. "That was not cool, not cool. I didn't give you permission, so you take it down. Now."

If he had been on the other side of the door, I would have called the police. This was not the Alex I knew. Well, actually, I only knew him on Facebook. Which meant I had no idea who he was.

I hauled out the laptop. Logged onto my blog account. Went to the post about Alex. Deleted it. Sent him a text.

> Me: did it.
>
> Alex: am still on ur list of friends
>
> Alex: delete it now
>
> Alex: now

I went to the section of the blog that listed all the friends I had met. I deleted his name. I decided to not text him back. I logged on to Facebook and defriended and blocked him. He sent me a text.

>Alex: it shows up on google. delete it on google.
>
>That I didn't know how to do.
>
>Alex: delete on google

Three days later, I got a message from a woman named Erin from San Diego.

>Erin: Did you sleep with Alex? Because he is my boyfriend. Or was my boyfriend. I read your blog. You are disgusting.
>
>Me: Alex was a Facebook friend with whom I played Scrabble. I never knew that he had a girlfriend, and I'm sorry for any hurt that I have caused you.
>
>Erin: He's a liar and a player. And he says that he never thought you were sexy. You are an ugly old lady according to him.
>
>Me: Yes, I am actually.

My status: vain, fading flower, easily swayed by flattery.

# August—Friends 187 through 206: Activity Recent

I had no idea who Terri was. But she was my Facebook friend. Although she had over a thousand Facebook friends, and—by this time in the year—I had just as many, we had no mutual friends. I couldn't remember why or when either of us had sent a friendship request. Over the course of the year, I sent her several messages and received nothing back until the beginning of August when she invited me (and every other of her thousands of Facebook friends) to a party at the Elyssian hotel. I RSVPed immediately and, when I got there, discovered a party totally devoted to my weakest nature.

The party was held in three ballrooms of the hotel. Trays of chocolate-dipped strawberries were passed, although there were no takers. There were, however, takers for the champagne. And the makeovers, the free manicures, the demonstrations of new and exciting dermatological and surgical techniques. There were social skeletons in expensive dresses, and I didn't recognize anybody. I located Terri at a booth demonstrating a line of moisturizers and creams. She was a likable enough girl, a little skittish when it became clear I wasn't here for the scripted pitch, and I had no idea who she was.

"We're Facebook friends," I told her.

"Okay," she said, drawing the word out for three extra syllables.

"And I don't know how we're friends."

She looked over my shoulder to see if anybody was going to save her, but no, she was on her own.

"I tend to look for friends on Facebook who are… open to what I do."

"What do you do?"

"I'm an aesthetician. I help women feel better about themselves. By looking better."

"So you look for Facebook friends who want to look better?"

Which is to say middle-aged women who are insecure and vain? In which case, sign me up. Which she didn't. Because a guest had elbowed her way in front of me to inspect the jars of moisturizer and Terri had an escape.

I started the year with friends in Hawaii, Seoul, Taipei, Manila, Mumbai, Dubai, Rome, Dortmund (Germany), and in England.

If I were Spielberg, I would take a toy plane and some pushpins and traverse the map in a westward direction, ending back in Chicago. Planning was something I did during the day. Worrying was what I did when I woke up in the middle of the night.

After how to pay for tickets, the most important question was whether I could persuade someone to go with me. Because the notion of traveling around the world was scary.

The first two people I asked were, of course, my two sons Joseph and Eastman. They both had good reasons to say no. Eastman was in college. Joseph had a job in New York. I tried to persuade Joseph that he should quit and use my trip as an excuse rather than telling his boss, "I hate this job because you're a jerk" but I didn't get any traction on that.

Between March and August, there were eight volunteers including eighty-two-year-old Judy Wilkinson. I decided to take a pass on her offer, mostly because I figured that I would have to carry her luggage and quite possibly her. Seven other people eventually found a new job, started school, got a new boyfriend or husband, and pretty soon, I believed I might have to do this on my own.

In August, I started e-mailing the international friends and trying to figure out who had conflicts. For instance, Facebook friend Cecilia who had been a teacher in my sons' schools had moved to the United Arab Emirates. She lived and taught at a school in El Ain, about an hour's car ride outside Dubai. She messaged me that I shouldn't try to rent a car and come to her. Instead, she'd come to Dubai, and we'd spend an afternoon together. But it should be on a Saturday.

And I received a message from Susan who was supposed to be in Hawaii.

> Susan: Didn't you pay attention to my earlier messages? I said I was going to Turkey to teach. I'm already in here. Outside Ankara.
>
> Me: I thought you said Tunisia. And I thought it wasn't until January.
>
> Susan: That was a different grant program. When are you coming?

Me: October. Can we meet in Istanbul?

Susan: No, you have to come here. I have classes. I am going to have you talk to my students about what it's like to be famous.

Me: I'm not famous.

Susan: You are on Facebook.

Me: Facebook is not the real world.

I opened another tab on my computer and looked at MapQuest. I would have to fly into Turkey from Dubai and then take a nine-hour train ride from Ankara to her university.

Susan: And can you bring with you a Mac and a printer? I can't get one shipped here.

I had learned to travel very light. I carried a Carharrt's utility bag that had lots of compartments. I always carried my laptop, a flip camera, and the William Clark plush toy that reminded me that I was not a wimp but an adventurer. I never checked a bag and could make do indefinitely with a change of underwear, three packs of Hanes t-shirts that were cheap enough that I could didn't mind tossing them if I couldn't jam everything back into the bag, and a cosmetic bag with DERMAdoctor MED e TATE individually packed deodorant, rollerball Angel perfume and sample size mascara and lipstick. I planned on taking just that and a sweater when I went overseas.

I thought about the projected itinerary. Chicago to Korea, Korea to Taiwan, Taiwan to the Philippines, Philippines to India, India to Dubai, Dubai to Turkey. From Turkey I would be heading for Rome where I figured I might buy a change of clothes for the second half of the trip.

I couldn't see how I could check a Mac and a printer at every airport without risking a baggage re-direct. No way could I manage to carry them in taxis and trains and buses without losing or dropping them. Knowing me, I would be on the flight out of Taipei and would remember that I had left them in the Taipei Holiday Inn room that morning.

Why couldn't I just order her one and have it shipped to her? I checked the Apple website. There didn't seem to be any problem with shipping to Turkey so I decided if I am buying it, I could get it to her any way I please. But I hesitated when I got to the checkout page. I hadn't seen Susan since college. We were the laziest of correspondents on Facebook.

Me: You need me to buy you a Mac and a printer?

She didn't reply.

Then I thought—I shouldn't have sent that text.

In late August, I got a phone call from a Chicago area code. I didn't recognize the number, and I let it go to voice mail.

"Hi, my name is Ann Corcoran and I'm with the *Rosie O'Donnell Show,* and we've been really interested in your story. We'd like to talk to you about coming on sometime in September. Could you give me a call back?"

I had been approached by media outlets, particularly in February when newspapers, magazines, and radio shows do "how's that New Year's resolution going?" features. I had done my share of laughing along with hosts at how silly my resolution was. I had clippings from the local paper with a picture that made me look fat and a caption that pegged me at four years older than I was.

There is nothing more flattering or seductive than the promise that you are beautiful and that you are going to be famous.

I called back. The producer squealed and gushed as if she truly thought that I was the greatest gal in the world. I was so profound. So funny. So wonderful. The world—and certainly Rosie O'Donnell herself—couldn't wait to marvel at me.

"I just have one last question," she said after we established that, yes, I could fit an appearance on her show into my busy schedule. "Can we talk to your doctor?"

"Why?"

"Well, the agoraphobia angle. I mean, you feel capable of doing a show, but just for legal reasons, we'd want to establish..."

Her voice trailed away, and I suddenly realized where she was going with this. She was concerned I might have a whopping anxiety attack on the show and maybe I'd die or be permanently injured.

I thought, *Yeah, of course, I've got a good chance of having the mother of all anxiety attacks, of having a heart attack, a stroke, any number of instantaneous deaths on television.*

I could stop breathing for any number of reasons or no reason at all. I could turn bright red with hives. I could say something mortifying. I could do all of that and more. Because over the course of the past eight months, I had done all of that.

In planes stuck on runways, in airports with cancelled on flight boards, in my car, before meetings with people I didn't know very well or knew not at all and for every new experience that someone wanted to "introduce" me to. I had done a lot of things that I couldn't have anticipated having the courage to do. So I figured all those recent activity posts? Everything had made me ready to say yes.

# September—Friends 207 through 231: Re-friending

Facebook uses everything—every photo, every video, every post, every link you put on your page. It uses your list of friends—even the friends who aren't on Facebook but who happened to be in the album you posted of "My Barbecue June 12." We probably should be alarmed. But we're having so much fun tagging our pictures and bragging about what we made for dinner that we haven't seemed to protest. We have given to Facebook its only asset—information about its users.

And cell phones? We should call them what they are: a GPS system for the government and for companies who would love to sell us something. If you go missing tomorrow or if you commit a crime, law enforcement can pinpoint where you are now and where you've been through your phone. And companies can spot which restaurants you looked for, what specialty shops you favor, with the same precision. The fact that you can phone and text with it is just an added feature to keep you interested and distracted.

I am not bothered by this. Perhaps because I figure that I am so absolutely boring in my habits that I will never attract the attention of any tyrannical force.

I went to my doctor in early September. The *Rosie* producers had sent me a release form.

"What are you going to talk about on the show?" my doctor asked. Dr. Stern is a sole practitioner with a lot of drug samples for every occasion. He's probably my age and prematurely gray, unless some of those drug samples do more than keep one's health.

"The Facebook project."

"You're still doing that?"

"It's a yearlong project."

"Oh. So what do you want me to say to the *Rosie* people?"

"Just answer whatever questions they've got. Except maybe you could leave out that urinary tract infection episode. I had never had one, so I'm still embarrassed about that episode."

"If I recall, you were mostly embarrassed at how you got it, not the fact that you had me paged at three o'clock in the morning."

"Girl's gotta have fun."

He signed the form and slid it across the counter.

"Honestly, you don't mind total strangers knowing anything about you? I know, I know, except for that UTI."

"If I was applying for health insurance, which I have to do pretty soon, I'd have to sign something saying you have to give them everything in my chart."

"Yeah, but insurance is different. You have to have insurance. You don't have to go on the *Rosie O'Donnell Show*. Which brings me back to the point, what do you want me to say? Because if you want to be on the show, I can answer the producer's questions one way. If you don't want to be on the show, I can answer them another way."

"This has been a year of strange things. I might as well play it out."

He stared at me.

"You have changed. Tell me when it airs."

"Oh, and I need vaccinations and shots."

"Where are you going?"

"Korea, Taiwan, the Philippines, Mumbai, Dubai, Turkey…"

"You? You're scared of flying."

"I'm scared of everything. But I'm getting a little better about that."

He mulled that over.

"Just make a list and leave it with my receptionist. And we'll have you come in next week."

The *Rosie Show* producers were adamant: I was not to post on Facebook about the upcoming taping, not to blog, not to even tell anybody. They wanted pictures and videos from the blog. They wanted better resolution pictures and videos from the blog. They had me scheduled for a Tuesday. No, Monday. Make that a Wednesday. At one o'clock. At three o'clock. They'd send a car.

At that time the comedienne was involved in a name calling public argument with Donald Trump. So I had several nightmares that involved being on television with Rosie O'Donnell and her calling me names. The nightmares never ended up with Donald Trump issuing a statement that I was an all right kind of gal.

One evening a few days before the taping, I checked my Facebook messages and saw that Susan had written. The issue of the Mac computer and how to get it to Susan had weighed on me. I knew how to ship a computer to the university where she taught but then had discovered that she wasn't listed anywhere as a professor, assistant professor, or even a graduate student assistant.

Dear Arlynn:

I can't believe what a hideous witch you are being. I would never ask someone to bring me a computer without paying for it. You can ask any of my friends and they'd tell you that I always pay my own way. In fact, I had planned on giving you a check for the full amount of whatever this cost you as soon as we saw each other. You never wanted to be my friend. And your New Year's Resolution isn't about friendship, it's all about you. You just want to be famous.

Susan

I felt a red hot blush. I hit reply. Facebook informed me that "the account that you are trying access is no longer available." She had blocked me. I went to my friends list. Susan was gone. Then I remembered that I had an e-mail address for her in my Hotmail account. I sent her an apology and offered to ship the computer to her, and we could worry about repayment later.

I felt attacked. Accused. But not unjustly. There was nothing she was saying that wasn't in the back of my head. Had I lost sight of the real value of friendship? Had the New Year's Resolution become an ugly selfish mess?

I wanted to drink a bottle of white wine to numb every bit of me and then get into bed and pull the cover over my head. Which I did. Although, to be fair, I watched some television. But mostly I thought about Susan.

Beginning at noon the next day, I was to be owned by Rosie O'Donnell. Not by her personally, I'm sure she had not the slightest interest in me one way or another. But I did exactly what I was told to do. Washed my hair but didn't apply any product (since I don't ever apply product, this was the easiest of the directives to follow). Didn't put on any makeup—I had up until this moment never left the house in my adult life without mascara.

But I felt an uneasiness that went beyond stage fright.

At twelve thirty, a black limousine pulled into the driveway. It was the last moment for me to back out. I could. It's not like they would sue me.

The driver honked the horn.

I walked out to the back porch. The driver stepped out of the car and looked at me. With what seemed to be disappointment. I was nobody he had ever heard of.

Which made me feel great!

I got into the car. The driver called ahead to the studio to say we were on our way. I took an Ativan. At the studio, a producer—everyone who works on a show, as near as I can tell, are producers—took me to a dressing room. On the door was a sign "Arylnn Presser."

A long mirror with lights, a small platter of vegetable crudités and brownies, and a selection of Diet Cokes, waters, and teas. A woman did my hair. And then told me that I wasn't supposed to touch it. Again. Ever. A woman did my makeup. And told me that I wasn't supposed to touch my face. Again. Ever.

Ben and Brandon showed up with the camera. We hadn't spoken or seen in nearly three weeks, although Ben had sent me several e-mails saying that this appearance on the *Rosie Show* would absolutely solidify investor money. He started to film in the hallway and was quickly ushered back into the room and told that he couldn't film in the hallway or in the dressing room. The producer left only after Ben put his camera back in the case.

"I don't see why you didn't stand up for me," Ben said. "This is totally the best thing that's happened to this project."

"I think I've lost a friend because of this," I said. "Not exactly because of this, but because of what a show like this means."

Ben and Brandon were taken into the studio to watch the taping. I was scheduled for a segment forty-five minutes into the show, immediately after Joan Cusack who would be promoting a new television series about a detective who is an agoraphobic and solves all the cases presented to her by means of deduction. And without stepping off her front porch.

And there was some kind of game show segment. A musical interlude. At five o'clock, a producer came in to tell me that the show was technically over, but that they would shoot my segment anyway as a "web extra."

"Is the audience exhausted?"

"They're a little tired. But we're paying them so..."

"And Ms. O'Donnell, Rosie, wants to do this?"

"Absolutely."

"Okay, well, then let's have at it."

I was shaking and unsteady in heels. The Ativan had worn off and nobody looked like they were going to offer me a preflight beer. A very nice stage manager walked me around the audience and onto the platform where Rosie O'Donnell herself was getting a makeup fix. As I slid into my seat, she paused to shake my hand and we chatted for a moment although I cannot remember about what. She had a genuine smile and I really liked her.

I don't remember anything about the next three minutes except this: the audience was the most animated group of people I had ever seen. When I said something sad, they sighed. When I said something even remotely funny, they laughed as if I were the most brilliant comedienne. I found out later they were paid.

The segment ended, and I was patted by the stage manager who led me back through the backstage area. Ben and Brandon were waiting in the dressing room.

"We should go get a drink to celebrate," Ben suggested. "Because we need to talk. This is a total game changer. You were articulate, you were funny, you were exactly what you needed to be. And when this airs, investors are going to be beating my door down."

"This isn't going to air."

"What do you mean?"

"The show was already over. They only filmed me because I was here, and who knows? Maybe some other segment was a wash and they'll use it. But that's a bit unlikely. And this entire afternoon wouldn't be airing until October and I'll be long gone."

"But I'm going with you."

"I'm sorry."

The producer came in again with a form for all three of us to sign.

"Just remember," she said. "No blogging about it, no mentioning the show, no Facebook references. And thank you. If it airs, we'll contact you. Oh, and the driver is waiting for you."

"Can't she just go across the street with us for a drink?" Ben asked.

"No, we really don't like to do that. Because we pay the driver by the hour."

I was shown out a door. The limousine was parked on the curb.

A few weeks later, I got an e-mail from Susan:

> Merhaba,
>
> Apology accepted. What is so incredible ironic is we as humans have become a product of our technology. We all tend to forget that technology is only as smart as the human operating the equipment. And we have all forgotten that we are thinking rational beings and not computers. We live in a technological world that has taken over our everyday thoughts and emotions. Facebook has changed our perception of the word friend and this just might be part of our evolution as human sapiens! Still battling that thought. What we have to be remember that anything can go wrong in the technological world. Really not sure

if you ever got the e-mail or Facebook message I sent explaining the different options for the computer purchase. I am not in America anymore and there is no such thing as instant gratification. I have no cell phone service at this point. Last night I found, on one of my iPhones, a message I sent you in my trash. To my horror I realized you may not have gotten this e-mail about the options.

I believe in Dunbar's number and the value of 150. I am leery of people who have more than 150 Facebook friends. How does one stay in touch with everyone and have any semblance of a relationship or friendship. We may not be primates but we have similar habits. Facebook has become more about inflating our egos rather than staying in touch with friends. We tend to lump friend with anyone that wants to exchange Facebook names. Is this a friend? I still believe a friend is someone we make physical contact with at least in the beginning.

Unfortunately we do not use the term "pen pal" which is what I believe Facebook is.

I find your project interesting however for me I would need to make a decision and distinction between people who are friends and people who want to be a friend because of fame. Facebook is becoming a very dangerous field in which we get sucked into the mindless unthinking world of cyberspace. Hope I haven't defriended you. Can't seem to figure out what is wrong with accessing you on Facebook. Merhaba

I closed the computer. Took a shower to get the makeup and hair product out. And then, I sat down to write one last plea to my older son Joseph.

Me: Quit your job, your boss is a jerk, and please come with me around the world. There aren't all that many times that you get to do such a trip. And besides, I really need you.

# October—Friends 232 through 246: Add Your Current City

Every day was a numbers game, a countdown to December 31 when I would either consider this a success or maybe a failure. Every morning began with two hours of meticulously messaging or responding to messages about upcoming meetings and about setting up my schedule. Scrolling through Orbitz, Priceline, Kayak, and other sites to find the cheapest rates on hotels, flights, rental cars.

I was getting friendship requests, some from people who knew me and some from people who had read about what I was doing. A lot of new friends wanted advice about how to get over anxiety attacks, how to get out of their houses. How to get visas to relocate to the United States. How to pay for an operation for their sick child. Marriage proposals. Business opportunities.

What could I tell them? Alcohol? Ativan? Working out until all your adrenaline is gone? Big extra thick crust pizzas and Pepcid for the acid reflux? Call the State Department?

A week after the Rosie Show taping, Joseph called me.

"I just gave my boss notice," he said. "So I can go with you. But when we get to England, there's some friends I want to see, so you're sort of going to be on your own some of the time."

"Thank you so much! This is going to be fun!"

"I don't know about that. But if I am the only one who is willing to go with you, I guess I have to do it."

I had missed him so much in the past years since he had gone to college and gotten a job. Now I felt like everything was exactly how I would have wanted it all year. The next few weeks were a flurry of immunizations, visa applications, packing, and repacking.

I started to feel something about travel that I would never have suspected: excitement, happiness, pleasure, anticipation.

All of the good emotions that are just the other side of the coin of fear, anxiety, dread.

On the afternoon I visited the Indian visa center in Chicago, I ran into Ben at an elevator bank. He carried his backpack with the camera and gear. We shared an awkward hug.

"Hey, how are you?" Ben asked.

"What are you doing here?"

"I'm getting a visa. I'm going to need one for when we get to India."

"You got the money to...?"

"No, but I've got some calls out and I am very optimistic."

"Good luck."

"Yeah, I need it."

He headed for the consulate offices. I respected that he was doing what I was doing: making a resolution, aiming for its conclusion, and hoping that all the forces of the universe would work to his favor. I knew he'd have to take that determination and make a success of his next project.

I also was a little relieved, because now it was just me and Joseph.

But I still had one more major trip before going around the world, and it was going to be a sprint.

There were two friends in Alaska. One was Christie, a teacher who had given up on romance and getting a decent job in Illinois and hoped that at the southwestern tip of Alaska, Homer, she would find both. The other Facebook friend was the Coglan's son Ian in Nome. Nome was unreachable by train or car, although there is a highway that runs out of town for about a hundred miles of nothingness.

I would leave Chicago on a Thursday and return from Alaska on a Sunday. Leave for Korea the following Sunday.

My chaperone for the Alaska trip was Deedge. I met him in fifth grade. We have sometimes veer into the romantic territory and sometimes into the "we're just barely speaking" land.

He wasn't on Facebook. He didn't own a cell phone. Except for checking on baseball stats, he hated the Internet He thought what I was doing was baffling and ridiculous. But he'd be happy to be my chaperone since he had always wanted to see Alaska.

Deedge drove three hours to Chicago so we could make a Thursday morning flight to Anchorage. We rented a car and drove five hours southwest to Homer. We took Christie to dinner.

Christie was Charlie's stepsister and I brought her greetings from the entire family. I admired her courage in making such a bold move. I had been to her going away party just a year before, and now she was as if a native Alaskan.

Deedge fell asleep immediately but he wasn't like Reggie. When I turned on the light to read a book, he protested. I turned off the light. Tried to sleep. Started to feel the niggling pain in my chest, the quickening of my breath, the sure knowledge that I was in Homer, and this was where I was going to die. After all, where was the hospital? Where was the Starbucks? Why was I so far away from home.

I walked out onto the parking lot. And looked up at the stars. There were so many more of them than in a Chicago North Shore sky—like being blanketed by Christmas lights. I felt small and alone, and I started to cry.

There were people partying on the second floor of the motel—windows open, music playing. Homer was a pickup and drop-off point for trucks going to and coming in to the United States from Asia and Russia. The people didn't know each other, but it didn't matter; everybody was a friend on this road. One man leaned out the window and asked if I wanted a beer.

"No thanks," I said. I think it's the only time in my life that I have refused a beer.

I moved farther toward the street and sat on the curb.

I crossed my arms up over my chest. I just wanted to be home. I would feel safe at home.

I wanted to stay in that safety forever.

But where was home now? The economy was squeezing enough that Stephen and I had dropped the price of the house again. If it didn't sell within the next few months, we were financially ruined. I had already prepaid the flights and hotels for the trip around the world, and there was no recovering that money. And I had lost what nest egg I would have taken away from the sale by banking on Ben.

And I had not been able to make my prayer of just imagining for a moment a God loving me as his own do anything more than keep me going for ten seconds at a time. The world is full of people who feel this way, who are lost and scared, and I was just one of them. Having a particularly bad night.

I gave in, gobbling a couple of dry Ativan and went back to the room. Time zones being what they are I had been up for close to twenty four hours. I thought I would never be able to fall asleep but I was quickly gone.

The next morning, Deedge and I drove back to Anchorage and picked up the flight to Nome. Alaska Airlines is like no other airline: the pilots are able to land on your front porch if that's all you'll give them, which it was about what they had for the brief layover on the Kotsebue Island.

And people use the airline like a New Yorker does the subway: it was Friday afternoon as a group of folks got on the plane at Kotsebue heading for Nome for a high school football team. The flight attendants knew everybody, and people gossiped and talked, shared whatever beer and chips they had brought onboard.

At Nome, Ian Coglan—newly minted as a missionary for the Covenant Church—waited in the terminal. Well, the room of the airport. He took us to the Airport Pizza, a company that uses a Cessna for deliveries.

Nome is a collection of bars and tanning salons, and everyone works on a different circadian rhythm.

The next morning, Ian took us on a tour of the village. We again ate lunch at Airport Pizza and went to the museum to look at a lot of taxidermied sled dogs. We went to dinner at a Korean restaurant with tables made of planks and a menu that was puzzling.

"What are you looking for?" Ian asked.

"Well, the owner is Korean, so I was expecting Korean food. Or something that is native to Alaska."

"Nome is completely cut off, and everything has to be shipped in. Get the cheeseburger. Everybody else is ordering it."

The restaurant had been overtaken by students who were taking part in a two-week vocational education program at Nome High School, which was designed to show them that there was a world outside of their tribal village.

"We're trying to tell them that they don't have to stay in their village," one of their teachers explained to me. "Today, for instance, Alaska Airlines sent someone to talk to them about getting jobs as baggage handlers or ground crew. For some of these kids it is a great ambition."

Then Ian drove us to the airport. My bag was pulled apart by TSA, and at the Anchorage Airport, when we switched gates, I was again yanked for a search. A six-hour flight back to Chicago in time for Sunday breakfast.

"You're going to have to be able to do this next week," Deedge pointed out. "Three weeks, and you'll be on a plane every other day."

"I'm going to need, like, six preflight beers to get on the Korea plane. And it's a nine a.m. flight."

"Chug."

I made another appointment with Dr. Stern and asked for sedatives with a little more juice to them, but he shot me down.

"You might be enormously high strung but you've managed a lot this year that neither of us would have expected."

Joseph returned from New York, and we packed.

The night before we were to leave, Joseph went out with friends. I paced the house. I tried to sleep. I ate ice cream. I drank white wine and tried to black out. I called everybody I knew, including Deedge, in order to say a last goodbye.

If I got on the plane, there was no way to go backwards. And not just because the tickets propelled us forward, westward evermore. No, I didn't have the money to buy a ticket back from Seoul, from Taipei, from India, or wherever it is that I would decide I had had enough. I was committed once I got onboard Asiana Airlines flight 235.

The airport was quiet, and the cab had no trouble stopping curbside. I got out and waited for Joseph to pay the driver. And that's when I saw Deedge standing at the entrance.

"What are you doing here?"

"I wanted to make sure you got on the plane."

"You drove three hours just to nag me about getting on a plane?"

"Yeah," he said. "And I'm glad I didn't have to drive back to your house to get you because the parking here is insanely expensive."

He and Joseph shook hands.

"Give me your credit card, I'll check us in," Joseph said.

"You get to go to the club lounge with your ticket," Deedge said. "Get settled in. It's going to be fun."

"Please."

"Get your preflight beer."

"But you drove all this way."

"I did it because I wanted to make sure you get on the plane. If you get on the plane, you can be proud of yourself for the rest of your life. And if you don't, you'll always regret it. We talked last night, you hardly remember it, you were drinking too much and that's something you gotta work on, but you need to get your beer buzz to get on this plane."

He had quietly, but surely, had been propelling us both towards the security line, Joseph coming up behind us with our boarding passes. As Deedge kissed me good-bye, he also gave me a gentle shove.

"Ma'am, can I see your passport?" the TSA agent asked me.

By the time I turned around, Deedge was gone.

Joseph and I went to the lounge. An impossible luxury, but one that I had thought was worth the extra fifty dollars because it was quiet and there was free beer. I chugged three of them while Joseph made himself plate after plate of breakfast foods.

Within the hour, we boarded the plane. It was a sunny morning. At first, I thought it was either the beer or some heretofore unknown racism on my part, but I couldn't tell any of the flight attendants apart. I would have twenty-two hours to figure out that the code of dress, hair, and makeup was such that Asiana Airlines flight attendants are meant to look exactly alike, right down to the color of their lipstick.

When the passengers were settled, the flight attendants came out to the aisles and stood at attention.

They bowed.

The pilot made an announcement in Korean.

"Oh, jeez," I said. "I guess we're really doing this."

"You've spent all year talking about it," Joseph said. "Now you're doing it. Just think of it as a roller coaster. And that you're a kid. And that you're excited."

And then the plane took off.

# November—Friends 247 through 268: Deactivation

Back in July, the 194th Facebook friend I scheduled to spend time with was Rett Britt. Rett lived in Winnetka and was a dabbler, one of those dads who has a garage band and competes in triathlons. He was also a photographer, and what he wanted to do with our Facebook time together was to take pictures at the Chicago half-marathon.

He picked me up at the house at the unbelievable hour of 5:00 a.m., and we snuck into the media tent at six fifteen. Rett had an unbelievable talent for making people think that not only had they met before, but they were close friends. It was an easy sort of charm. And he never used it for evil purposes, unless you consider getting a press pass an evil purpose.

We positioned ourselves on an empty bridge—Rett was now the only "official" photographer—overlooking the thousands of racers at the starting gate. He put together his equipment and started clicking.

"For these people, their job is done," Rett said.

"They look like they're just getting started," I said.

And to be fair, a group of fidgeting, stretching, jumping, adjusting-their-gear runners don't look like they would believe themselves to be done.

"All the work is done. They've gotten up all the mornings and ran when they didn't feel like it or when they had other things asking for their attention. They've worked through the injuries, figured out what shoes work, stretched, and cross-trained and whatever. And now, everything here—the tents, the volunteers, the road itself—it's all here to celebrate what has already happened. This is just the fun part. The dessert."

The gun fired, the runners bolted up under the bridge, and Rett took pictures that he would later sell to runner's magazines.

And as the Asiana flight rumbled down the runway, I tried to pretend I was engrossed in my copy of *Vogue*. But I was scared. There was no way to get off the plane. No way to turn around and come back home without trouble. I felt my breath heaving up inside my throat. The beer buzz was gone. Joseph took my hand.

"I'm okay," I lied.

And then I thought about what Rett had said. I had done the work necessary for this part of my Facebook New Year's resolution. I had my datebook full of notes—flights, phone numbers, addresses, confirmation numbers. My Cartharrt's tool bag had my passport; my passport had the necessary visa stamps. My body was awash in vaccinations and inoculations. I was carrying bills in eleven different currencies—I knew I had barely enough for cab fare into Seoul from the Inchon Airport and probably far too much money for a day and a half in the Philippines. I had confirmed and reconfirmed with cheery and no doubt annoying e-mails to every friend.

I had done the work, and I would never be this age, at this moment, at this starting gate. I really hoped the pilot knew what he was doing because it was time for me to let go.

I can't say that I did a great job of it, but I managed. I read magazines, watched a movie, leaned over Joseph's arm, and made him show me an animation short that he spent the entire flight creating, puzzled over *bibimbap*, and watched the screen on the seat in front of me as it showed the plane going right over Alaska (Hey, Christie! Hey, Ian!) and gently curving over the Pacific Rim. Then veering out a comforting distance from North Korea's airspace and then gliding towards the Incheon Peninsula.

The airport was exactly like any airport I had been through in the last six months. There was a line. We joined that line, certain that everybody else knew what they were doing and we were the only idiots. I had always told my sons that they should thank me for two things regardless of how bad of a mother their future therapist might tell them I was—I had raised them with English as a primary language, and they had an American citizenship.

I don't mean that as a mean thing or some form of disrespect to other languages and nationalities. But you have to work to find an airport where you can't find someone who speaks English.

And there's so many people who want to enter America and live in the country that Joseph and Eastman will always have at least one means of getting a wife.

We got through customs even though I was not quite ready to bring out my Korean hello, mostly because I had already been told that the way I pronounce hello in

Korean is roughly the way most Koreans say "What is your problem?"

And then we went to the terminal where I had, in the course of eight e-mail exchanges, agreed with John Choi that we would meet.

"Who is this guy again?" Joseph asked.

"He's a guy I dated four times, maybe five. He was really was nice but you know."

Joseph looked at me. We had never discussed dating. Or specifically, me dating.

"In any event, he moved back to Korea. I mean, he wasn't raised in Korea, but he came back to be with family and he's, well, there he is."

John wore a black suit and crisp white shirt. A light blue tie. We hugged hello and I introduced Joseph. John guided us out of the airport to the cab stand.

*He never wore a suit when we went out*, I thought, just a little puzzled. I initially concluded that people in South Korea are just more formal in their dress, but leaving behind the airport, I realized it was just because we had met John at the terminal exit where the pilots and flight attendants gathered.

No, there was something else at work. John took the notion of someone flying in from Chicago very seriously. Sure, we were only going to have dinner and I was half asleep. But it was an attitude I had noticed in Alaska—at the time, I was the only person from the lower forty-eight states to visit either Ian or Christie—and I would encounter it next in Taipei when we would finally meet Warner Sills who was studying at the National Taiwan University. Making the trip encouraged a sense of the importance of friendship. It was more than a poke, more than a like, more than a comment on a status.

John ordered off the menu for us at a restaurant near the hotel where Joseph and I were staying overnight. We discussed the possible sale of a violin he had inherited—a sale that would be handled through a dealer who was a Facebook friend of mine. We talked about his upcoming trip to Chicago and compared schedules. I felt like Cinderella at midnight when Joseph reminded me that in less than six hours, we would be getting on a flight to Taipei.

The night before we reached Manila, I got a message from Mark Del Rosario. Mark had been the one to send me a picture of a roasted pig at the beginning of the year, and I had really looked forward to meeting him. He was a fan of my grandfather's writing, and I knew we would have stuff to talk about.

> Mark: This is Nona, Mark's wife. I am writing on his account because you must know that he has just been in surgery today to remove his appendix. I hope you can understand that he cannot meet you. Sorry.

"Oh, shit, what do we do now?" Joseph asked.

"I wonder if it's really Mark. Or is his wife upset that he's meeting with me. Because I don't even know her and we're not friends on Facebook. Maybe she feels left out. Or maybe this is just an excuse."

"It doesn't matter whether it's an excuse or whether it's true or whether it's his wife or not. You can't know the truth of that, but we have to figure out what to do."

"We fly to Manila. Because if we don't go to Manila, we can't make the flight to Kuala Lumpur, and if we don't do that, we can't get the flight to—"

"Okay, okay, fine."

"We'll have a good time."

"I don't know about that."

> Me: I'm sorry, Mark and Nona, about the appendix. Please get well soon and I hope to catch up with you another time.

We got on the flight, and in Manila, we took a cab from the airport to Quezon City and checked into the hotel. Joseph's room looked out over the metropolis—all skyscrapers and broad streets, fast cars, and billboards. My room was on the other side of the hallway and across the river was a shanty town with corrugated steel sheet roofs. I put my bag down on the bed and thought about how wonderful a nap would feel. The phone rang.

"This is the front desk. There is a woman here in the lobby who has been waiting for you for nearly two hours. Will you see her?"

Joseph and I went downstairs. A diminutive woman with sharp, intelligent eyes and a "you can't have a bad day if she smiles at you" smile waited for us. Nona Del Rosario introduced herself.

"I'm so happy to meet you," she said. "And Mark is so sorry to not be able to see you. If you don't mind, I'm here to take you out to see the city."

I didn't get to meet Mark, there was no roast pig, but it was a wonderful day. I made a new friend, not the friend I expected but a friend for life. Christmas season was just beginning and we marveled at the decorated trees.

The next morning, Joseph and I flew into Kuala Lumpur. From there to Mumbai. In Dubai, we met Cecilia and her fiancé. We walked through a bazaar and played with a hawk.

Everywhere, I learned what an idiot I am. How terrifically sheltered by the American Midwestern way of doing things. And the thinking that how I do things is the right way. Except, in general, playing with a hawk without wearing thick leather gloves is a bad idea and I think we can all agree on that.

In Rome, we went to the Coliseum and stopped at every church and cemetery. We spent an enjoyable dinner with Federico Cenci who had written his dissertation on my grandfather. It was particularly fun because I had helped Federico with his research. It seemed like all the planning had come to work out just fine.

But, in the back of my mind, I was worried just a bit about Claudia Klose. Claudia lived in Dortmund, Germany. In order to reach her the next day, we would take a train out of Rome, catch a flight to Vienna, change to a flight to Dusseldorf, and then another train to Dortmund. With incredible precision, we were to meet at exactly seven o'clock at the train station.

I had never met Claudia. I wasn't even entirely sure why we were Facebook friends. Her Facebook posts were almost exclusively in German. Our mutual friends included Ben and a director who had once used Eastman in a movie. I had contacted her many times, and she had often said that she was nervous about meeting me because she didn't think her English was very good. I figured that wasn't a problem since my German was confined to *nein*.

She said she was generally someone who didn't get out much. I said I was happy to just go for a walk with her, have some coffee, do the universal girl thing of shopping. Much of the trip was planned around her work schedule when she said she'd meet me after work for a walk around town.

In Rome, I composed a message to reassure her again that this wasn't meant to be a pressure-filled meeting. In fact, I hoped she'd just sit down for coffee or maybe walk with us around the downtown area. I kept trying to put her name on a message. And her picture would briefly pop up and then disappear. I went to my friends list. She was no longer a friend.

She had defriended and blocked me.

I went to Ben's profile. She wasn't listed as his friend any more. Same with the director.

"I think I scared her," I told Joseph.

"I could message her on my account," Joseph suggested.

We logged out of my account and logged into his. He looked up Claudia Klose. She didn't exist on Facebook. She had deactivated her account.

"Do you have an e-mail address for her?"

"I think so, but that's going to veer off into stalking. I think she just got spooked. I wish she would have done it before I booked the flight."

"What are we going to do?"

"We're going to Dortmund for absolutely no reason at all."

"Why can't we just change our flight to go directly to England? We'll just be there a day early."

I thought about what had happened when Mark had gotten his appendix taken out.

"We're going to Dortmund."

We took the train from Rome to the airport, flew into Vienna, spent a few hours waiting for the connecting flight to Dusseldorf, and then took a train into Dortmund. When we arrived at the station, we waited for a half hour at the agreed-upon meeting place just in case Claudia would change her mind. She didn't.

We walked to the hostel. I was utterly depressed and defeated.

The next day, we went to a medieval fair and watched the city workers put up what Dortmund claimed was the world's biggest Christmas tree. We shopped, drank beer, visited a church that had been rebuilt after World War II. I bought a pair of shoes, having destroyed the ones I had brought and having suffered from bleeding blisters for too long. It was a fun day, and maybe it was better because I didn't have a Facebook friend I was supposed to meet. Maybe some relationships are meant to be just for Facebook.

Late in the afternoon, we took a cab to the airport. Got on an Easy Jet flight bound for Luten, England.

If there is one thing I can recommend, don't ever fly Easy Jet. It was a scrum at the gate because there is no assigned seating and the airline always overbooks. We managed two seats. The flight itself? Alaska Airlines pilots would be ashamed and appalled at being labeled as in the same profession. And never ever book a room in an Easy Hotel after a flight like that. Easy Hotel, owned by the same folks, was like a dorm room in Depression University.

But I had arrived in England for the best part of the year, and so I don't really begrudge the Easy people. We traveled by train through Brighton and Southampton. And in Bristol, we met more friends and then onward to Eastbourne.

They say that everybody's profile picture is a lie. That's pretty much true, but in this case, there was no doubt. I got off the train and waved at the man at the end of the platform.

Mark Cage. I had at last met him, almost a year after.

We shook hands and then, laughing, hugged each other.

"So my girlfriend Laura is cooking a little something," he said. "Typical English dinner. Roast chicken, potatoes, brussel sprouts, bread pudding, a pie. It's a big deal you coming out here. But we have time for a drive first. To Beachy Head."

Beachy Head was a tall limestone cliff overlooking the channel. Joseph could walk within ten feet before deciding he'd rather step back. I crawled on the grass to the edge because it was so far down. And as Mark explained, it was where people came to commit suicide. It was beautiful and horrific at the same time.

"I understand that patch of time after I broke up with that girl was part of the reason you started this project," he said.

"Yeah, I mean I didn't do much."

"You were nice. Thank you."

"More like thank you. You made me start thinking about this resolution. I've seen a lot. I've gotten closer to my son." Both of us looked back at Joseph. "And I've met a lot of my friends, made my peace with some, learned a lot. It's been a really good year."

"Come on. We've got time for one beer before dinner. And it's a big dinner. You'd better have brought an appetite."

"I brought a twenty-three-year-old. That's an appetite for both of us. And I'm happy for you."

"I'm happy for you too."

# December—
# Friends 269 through 289:
# Not Just Facebook Friends

I at least wanted the Asian F.
I had begun the year with 324 friends and 365 days in which to meet them. Mathematically, that looks pretty doable. A friend a day and six weeks de vacannes in the south of France.

But some people stood me up. Some people were impossible to get a hold of. Some people were traveling. Some people turned out to be dead or spambots. And some people—well, me—turned out to have an occasional breakdown that involved a ladies' lunch of white wine followed up with television, popcorn, more white wine, and then a restless night's sleep on the couch.

At December 1, I had over fifteen hundred Facebook friends. Facebook is like a spider web that builds itself outward, and friends of friends and friends of friends of friends were sending friend requests. I always accepted with a cut and paste explanation of my New Year's resolution. I repeatedly posted, messaged, commented on the rules of my resolution—that I was obligated to meet the original 324 (okay, 325 friends). Some new Facebook friends didn't understand this limitation and assumed I was coming to Brazil, Japan, Chile, Nigeria, wherever they were. But pretty much everybody understood.

Many new Facebook friends told me stories of how they couldn't leave the house because of anxiety attacks, how they felt limited, how they wanted to meet their friends, how they spent too much time on Facebook and were worried they didn't have a life. The stories were heartbreaking because each one was a tragedy that was completely at odds with their cheerful Facebook profile pictures and the status updates. I did my best to respond to everybody, but I noticed that I could have cloned myself and spent every day in a Starbucks in front of my laptop fully caffeinated, and my message folder would still be full.

I recognized that I wasn't going to hit 100 percent. Just not possible. But now I was aiming for 90 percent. That would be completely respectable and would mean I had done my absolute best. An A minus. What my kids called an Asian F.

I hit New York a third time. I did another road trip through the upper Midwest. I was so proud of myself for solving the Wesley Facebook problem:

Wesley was a friend of my ex-husband's girlfriend. She was my Facebook friend, and I had asked her who Wesley was and why was he my friend. After all, during a brief hiatus from seeing my ex, she had married, and I thought perhaps I had met Wesley at her wedding. He listed himself as working for the Methodist church. Had he officiated?

"ArLynn, I'm Jewish," she exclaimed. "I met him at a party, and he friended me the next day. I accept everybody's friendship request because of business. Then he started being really aggressive about wanting to see me at my apartment. Not going out. Just the whole 'I'll bring over a bottle of wine and we'll get to know each other' business."

"Married," I guessed.

We both nodded.

Every couple of weeks, Wesley would invite himself over to my home. I always demurred, and my suggestions of coffee at Starbucks or a newly opened restaurant were rejected. Then I wouldn't hear from him until the next time that he invited himself over. This had been happening for more than a year, and it was simple background noise to my Facebook page.

But one Sunday evening, I had houseguests—a couple who were displaying their wood carvings at a weekend art fair. They were tired and had no real interest in meeting a Methodist minister Facebook friend, but they would be in the house.

To be fair, I explained the project to him. Invited him to look at my blog. But I never got any indication that he was anything other than devoted to his mission. His mission being in my house.

Wesley called to say he was on his way. He wanted to know what kind of wine I preferred. His excitement was palpable.

It struck me, not for the first time this year, that Wesley and I weren't friends. We weren't going to be friends. He could poke, he could like, he could comment and message, and I could do the same for him. But this was going to be an awkward evening, and there would be no good way this could end.

"And my friends are going to be so happy to meet you," I said. "I have houseguests."

"That's wonderful," he said. "I'll get an extra bottle and be there in about forty-five."

*I had really misjudged him*, I thought. I asked my guests if they'd be able to join us. They were pretty okay about it but wanted to change. I made some finger food snacks and put them on the living room table and brought out the scented candles. I started a fire in the fireplace. The Christmas tree looked great.

Three hours later, my houseguests went to bed. I blew out the candles and unplugged the lights on the tree.

The next morning, I messaged.

> Me: what happened?

> Wesley: my nephew got picked up for speeding and I had to bail him out.

I have never met Wesley.

At the beginning of December, I knew I had one last major trip. And since my father Justin insisted he wanted to travel with me, I invited him.

Justin had been switched from Ropinirole to another medication and his symptoms had completely disappeared within a few days. He had no memory of our February visit or the altercation that concluded that visit. We had played a lot of Scrabble over the course of the year and I figured we could do this.

I told him my last trip would include Bruce Byfield, an occasional writer whom Justin had known for years. He was in Vancouver, British Columbia. From there, we'd travel to Seattle to meet George, a high school friend—although to be fair, I was pretty sure that he had me confused with someone else. And then, there was Maggie, a law school classmate of mine, who was in Eugene, but had offered to drive into Portland because I was meeting Karen, a friend from high school.

"I can only spare three days," Justin said. "I'm going to New York for Christmas."

"It's still doable. We'd meet in Vancouver on Friday the sixteenth and see Bruce," I told Justin on the phone. "Take the Amtrak bus to Seattle the next morning. Then you fly directly back to Tallahassee through Atlanta and I'll continue onto Portland."

"Will you take care of booking everything?"

"I'm a pro. I'll send you confirmations tomorrow."

In December of the previous year, I had been someone who had never even purchased an airline ticket on her own, and now I was devising itineraries in my head and on my laptop. Yes, yes, I did originally book the Amtrak bus from West Vancouver in the U.S.A. which is actually not in the same country as Vancouver, British Columbia. But after fixing all that, I still had a workable schedule. Justin would fly out of Tallahasse and I would fly out of Chicago.

The afternoon of the sixteenth, Justin met me outside the United terminal at Vancouver airport. He was a little more frail than I remembered, but he seemed genuinely happy to see me. We took a cab into the city and checked into the hotel. Went to a nearby museum of First Nations art. I was delighted by the Christmas decorations and the smell of salty ocean and crisp spruce.

We had dinner with Bruce, and the two men exchanged memories. Justin even tried absinthe, made in the Czech way with sugar caramelized with a blowtorch. The next morning, we went to the station.

I had come to divide cultures into two types: ones that encourage standing in lines and those that encourage scrums with no clear rules and a lot of jostling. Canada is a country that has both those cultures represented in its British and French heritage.

The people gathering at the Vancouver bus station were roughly divided into equal groups. One looking as if they were raised by scrum people. The other looking as if they had been raised by people who got mad at people who jumped the queue.

"I like to sit in front, right behind the driver," Justin said as we surveyed the group. "Otherwise, I throw up. It's the prostate medicine."

One thing the year had taught me was flexibility in the face of new developments.

"I want you to look particularly frail," I said. "In fact, could you stoop over a little?"

The bus approached the curb. As it stopped, the doors opened. Definitely scrum behavior, but I was pretty determined to not arrive in Seattle smelling like vomit. After all, I only had two more Hanes t-shirts in my Carhartt's bag.

"Excuse me, pardon me," I said as I pushed Justin ahead of me like a human shield. "My dad is very frail. My dad needs some extra help getting into his seat."

We scored the seat he wanted. I put our bags in the overhead bin and sat down next to him.

"I liked that," he said.

"What? Having a last lifeboat on the *Titanic* experience?"

"No, you called me Dad. I liked that. You should do it more often."

I had changed a lot during the year. I had learned to be patient with travel. To pack a single bag to last three weeks. To sleep on an airport bench. To tolerate and even like things my friends did and said that weren't what I would have done or said.

But I know one thing about me didn't change. I wanted to be someone's friend. I wanted to be someone's mother. I wanted to be someone's everything.

And I wanted to be Justin's daughter. It couldn't happen just playing Scrabble on Facebook with him. I had to put more into it. I had to put more into all the relationships I valued. Facebook could only help. It couldn't be the only means of communication.

We met George to see the Seattle Christmas festival. I'm pretty sure that I wasn't who George thought I was. Afterwards, I had to pick up a train to Portland. Justin had to get to the airport. We hugged, and I said, "I love you, Dad." That was enough to embarrass us both. But I'm glad I said it.

Then he was off in a cab, and I walked through the downtown to the station.

I felt pretty damn good.

New Year's Eve should have been a party. Instead, I was happy to get into bed and watch television as I drifted to sleep.

289 friends. One less than an Asian F.

Just one more and I would have made 90 percent.

# Epilogue—Friend 290

I had admired Frank ever since I met him. Tall, lean, poignantly out, a figure in Renaissance Faire costumery. He had worked with my son Eastman on a show and had been nice to him. Which is a total friend for life thing for me.

But I hadn't physically seen him for years when I started to notice a series of posts from Frank in late 2010.

A group of posts about dental surgery. I noticed he was going in for bridges, caps, root canals. He was posting about weight loss and exercise goals. I sent him a message asking what was going on.

> Frank: I have been unhappy with my looks for a long time. So I'm doing something about it.
>
> Me: I've always thought you look great.
>
> Frank: Yeah, but I'm in a community that's pretty brutal about looks. And it makes me uncomfortable.

On January 2, 2012, I went to the Mary Ann's hamburger place in the Andersonville neighborhood. It was crowded, but I scored a table where I could watch the door. I didn't see Frank until he was standing right next to the table.

"Jeez, you really *do* look great!" I exclaimed and then immediately apologized. "I'm not saying you didn't look great before."

"Shut up!"

We sat down, and he told me an amazing story about making the decision to utterly change himself. He had reached an "I don't like this about me" moment, and the previous New Years, instead of saying "I'll learn to accept myself," he had figured out everything he needed to become the Frank he wanted to be. He made a New Year's resolution to become that person. Complete reorganization of his teeth that changed his smile, weight loss and exercise to make his body worth a couple of checkouts from men at other tables.

"I got a new wardrobe, I color my hair," he said. "I changed *everything*!"

"I'm just so surprised!"

"And I'm sorry I kept putting off meeting you. It's just you blog and put up pictures on Facebook, and I couldn't face you until I was ready."

"That's okay. I understand. You're better than the last 10 percent of my friends."

"You didn't make the Asian F?"

"No, one off. I said I would do it in one year and I missed by one person."

"Not quite. You know my job is in banking. Our year-ends were due December 31. I was at the office until just before midnight. Went home and fell asleep. And nobody, but nobody wanted to party last night. Instead, tonight—January 2—is my personal New Year's Eve. I'll be out drinking champagne like I've crossed the international date line for finance people. And then I'll make this year's resolution."

"So what does that mean?"

"It means you did make the Asian F. You are seeing Facebook friend 290. Exactly 90 percent."

"That's sort of cheating."

"It's your resolution. You can do whatever. And what's your resolution for this year?"

"I don't have one. I guess I should lose five pounds. I could do that. Except it's too small of a resolution. I wouldn't be as demented about making sure I did it."

"Make no small resolutions?" Frank suggested.

Make no small resolutions.

Rely on your friends for help.

Recognize the obstacles you put in your own way.

Be ready for surprises.

"Yeah," I said. "That just about sums it up."

⸻

Since I started meeting my Facebook friends, I have gotten a lot of new friends. And I've managed to meet a number of them because I think that it's very important to get out from behind the computer. And for someone like me, especially important to get out from under fears, anxieties, and the temptation to stay at home drinking white wine and watching television. Mark Zuckerberg, you've created a really cool way for friendships to flourish. And you've got over one billion people logging on. Thanks!

an extra special thanks
to
my Facebook friends!
to read all about each and every friend
visit, go to arlynnpresser.com

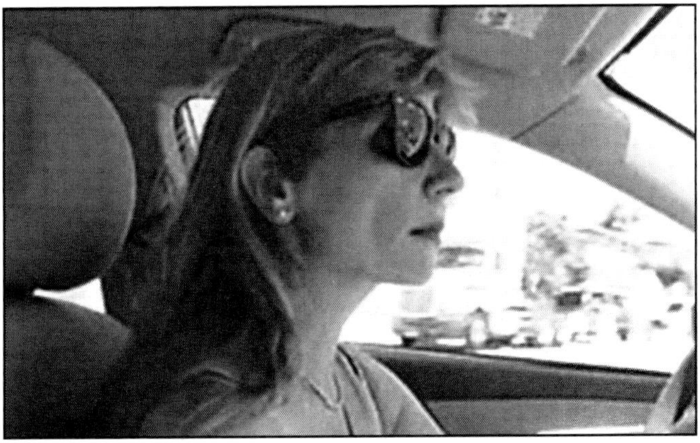

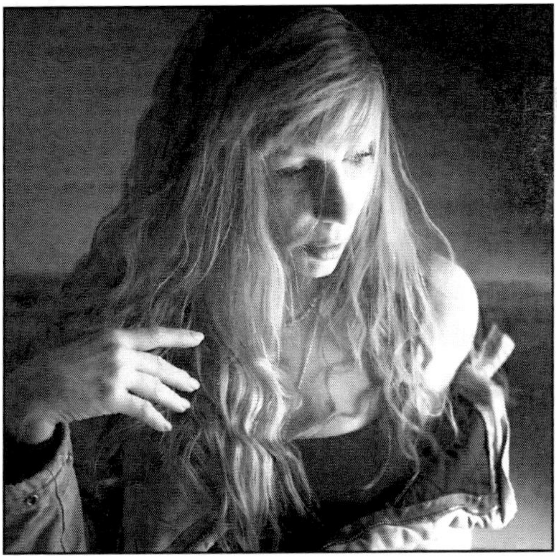

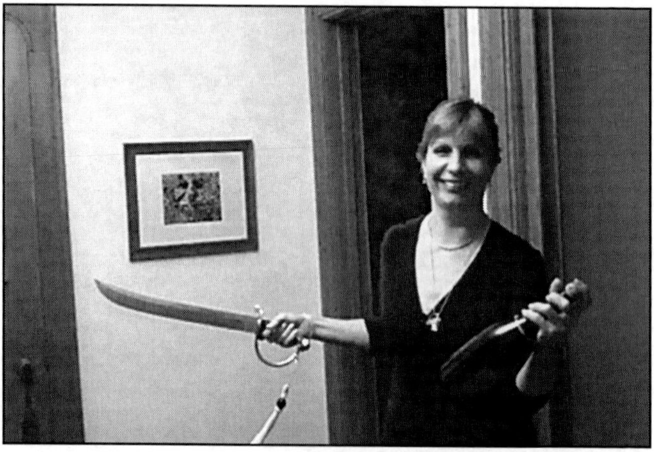

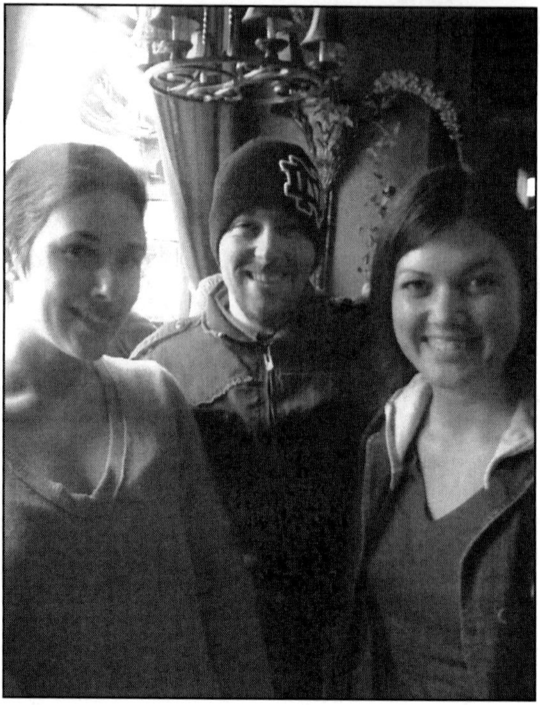

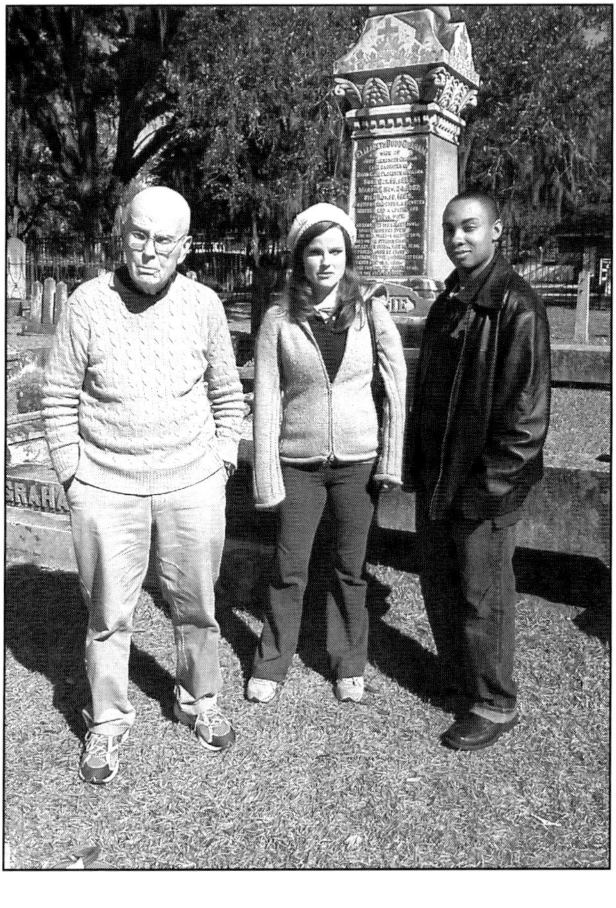

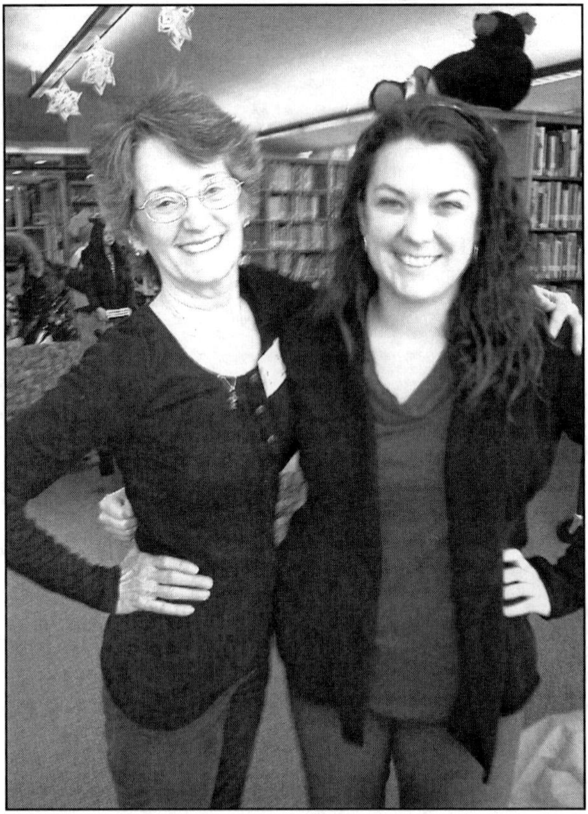

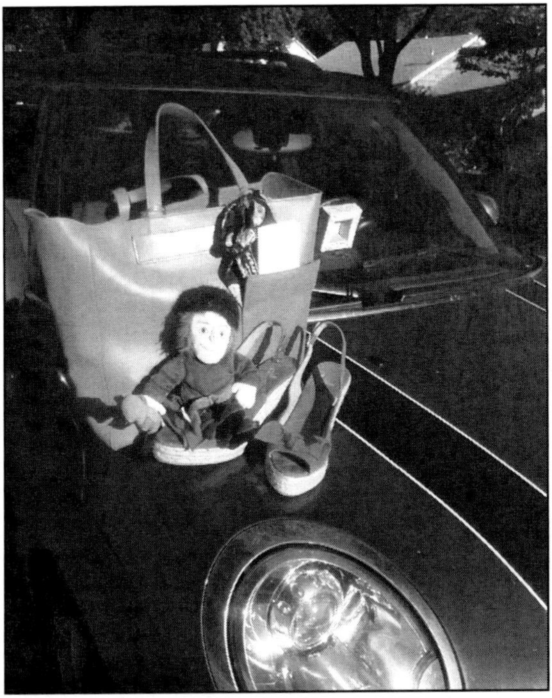

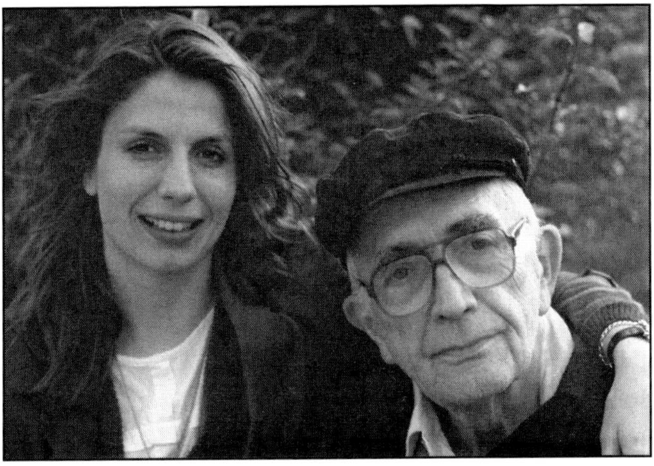

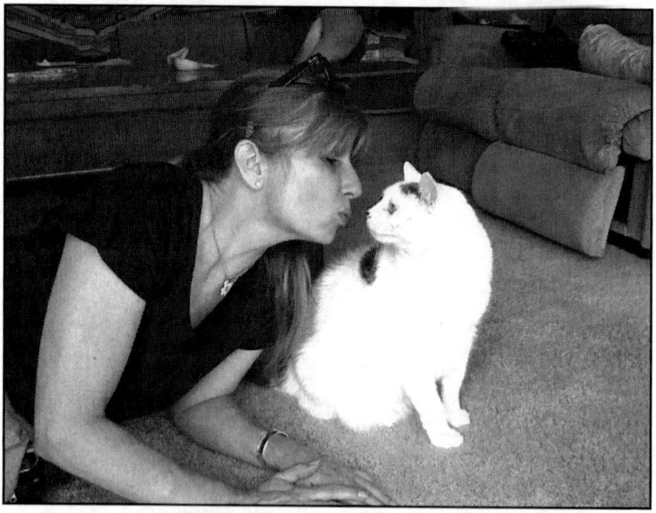

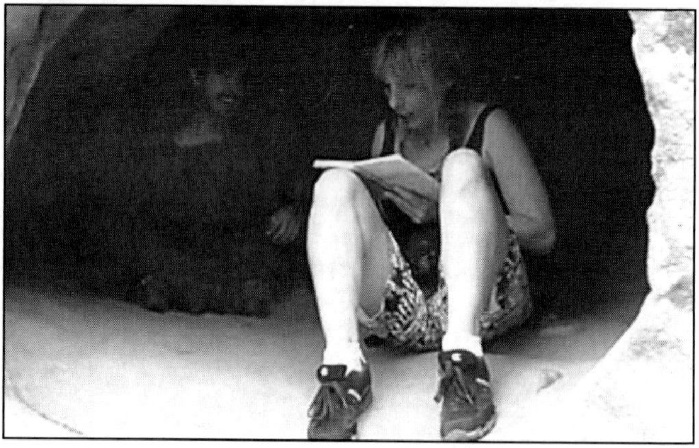

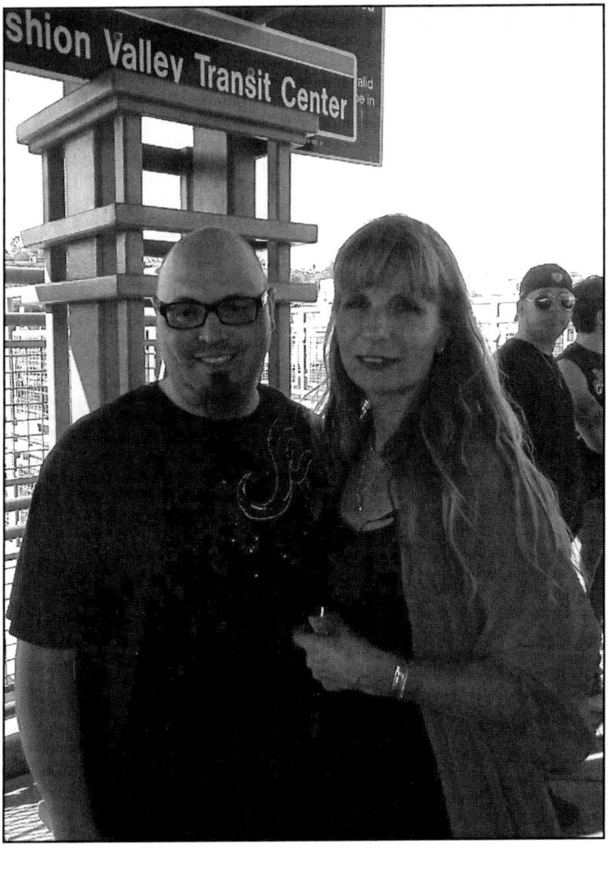
shion Valley Transit Center

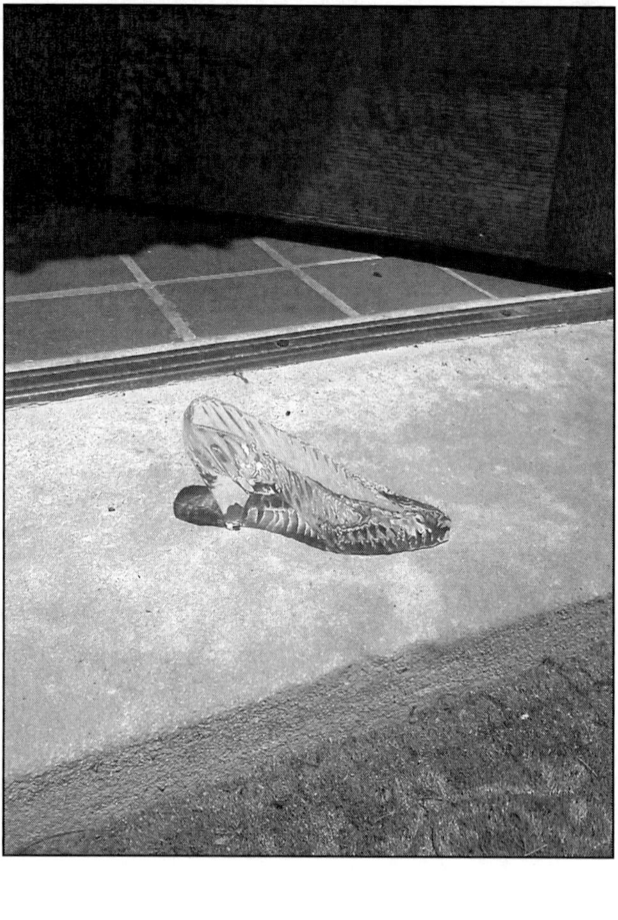

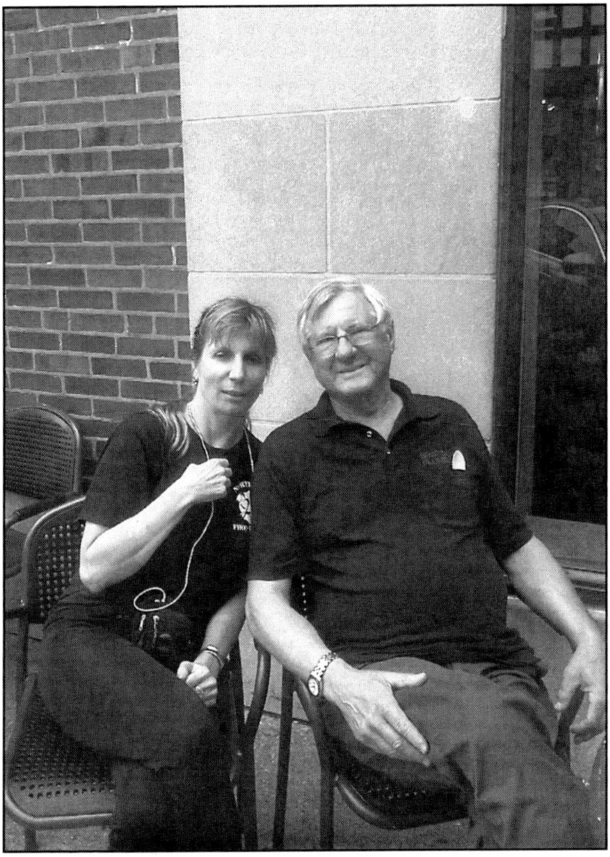

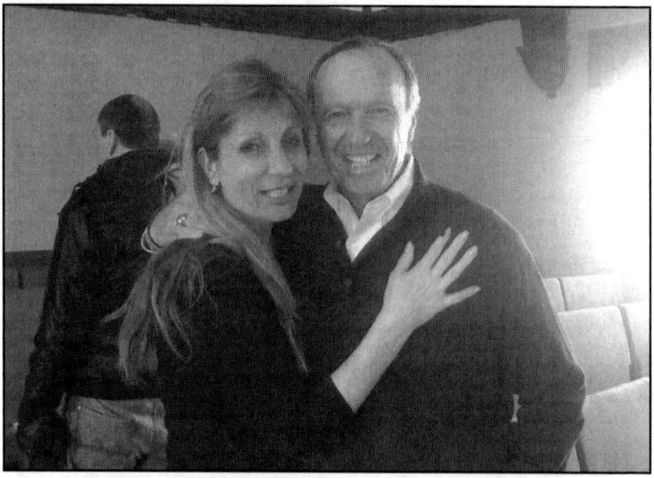

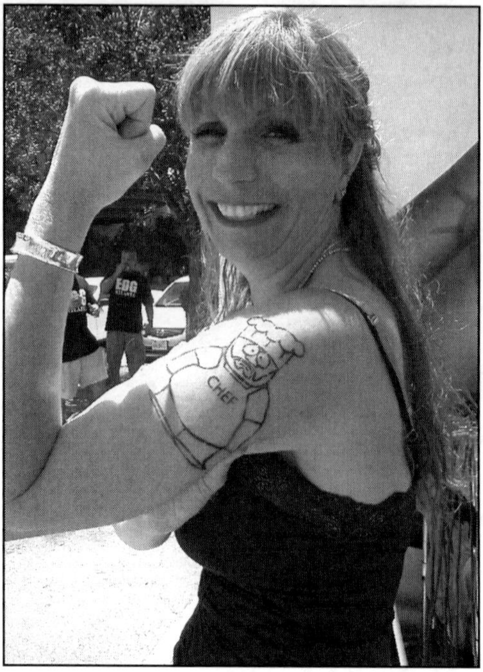
CHEF

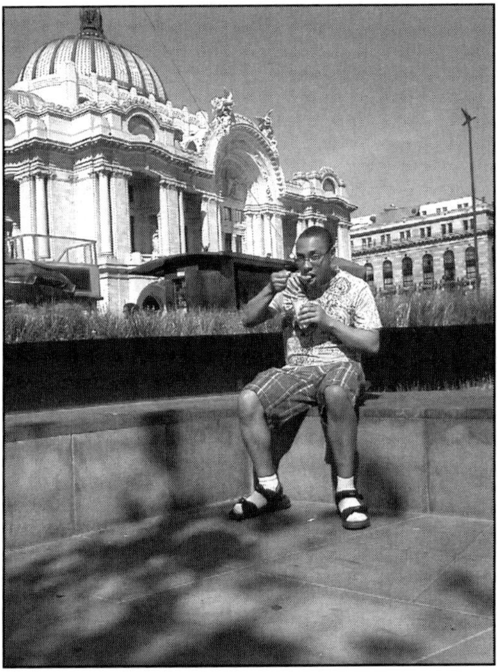

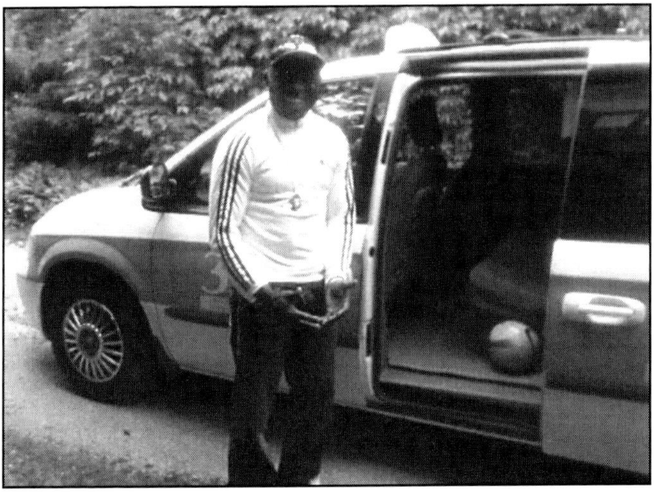

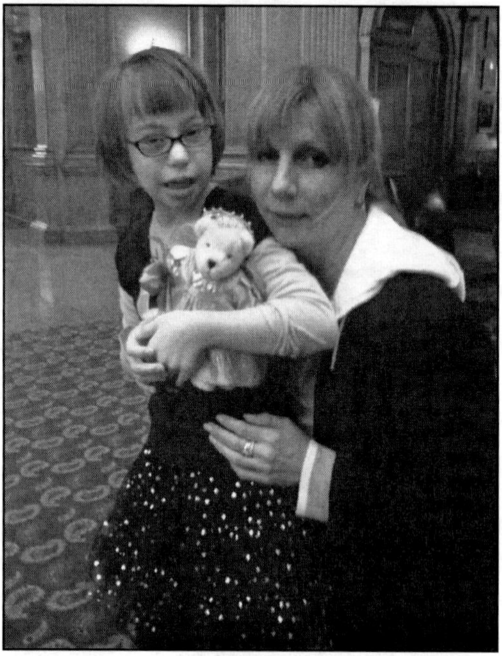

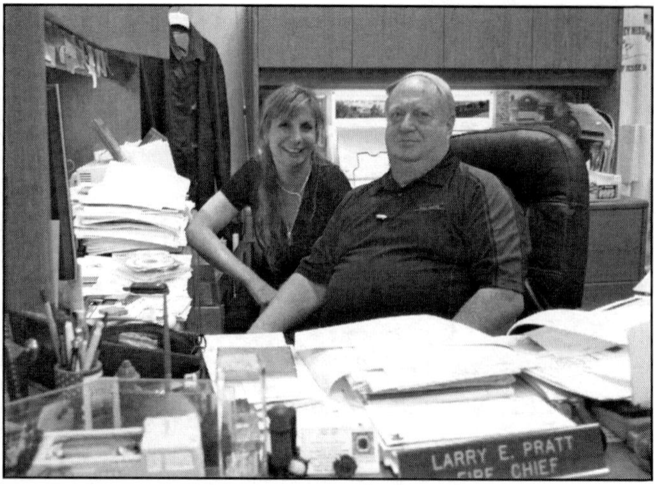
LARRY E. PRATT

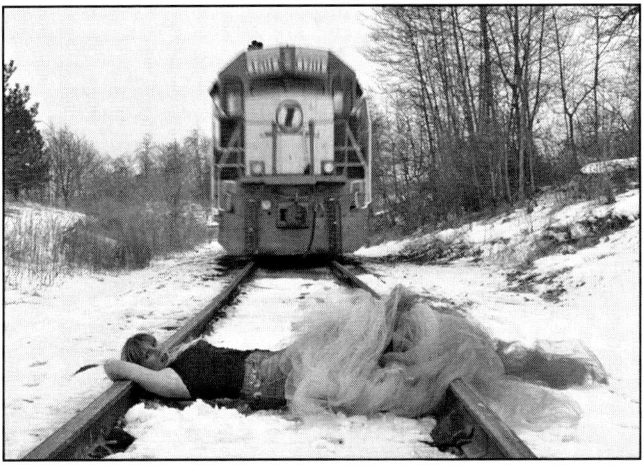

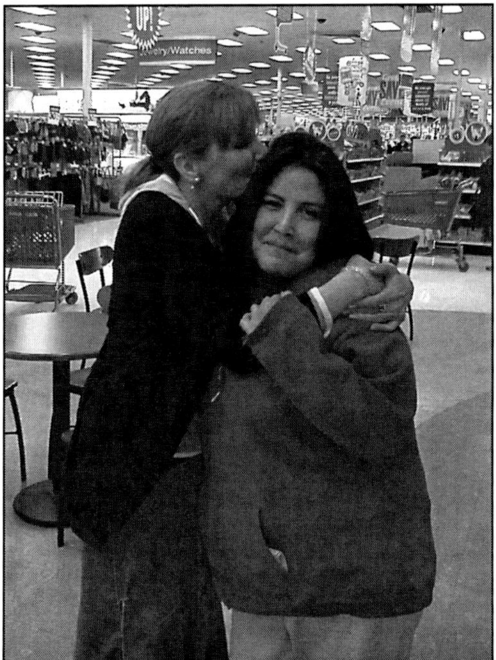

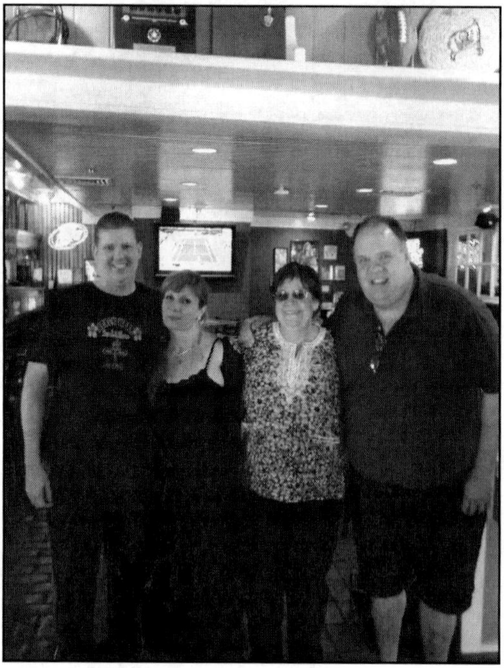

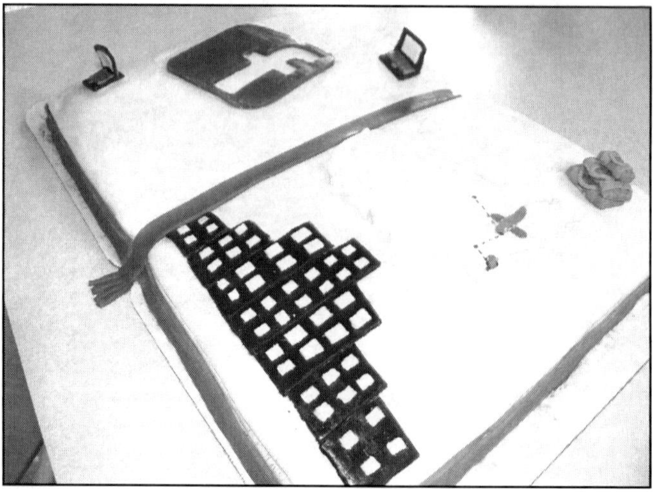

At a shrine for cabbies in Mumbai with Facebook friend Anto Prashanth

Grace Neuman taught ArLynn how to pop a champagne cork with a Cossack sword

# AMAZING FACEBOOK *ODYSSEY*

## Woman beats panic attacks to meet 'friends' around the world

ARLYNN PRESSER made a New Year's resolution to visit all 325 of her Facebook friends, a daunting task for anyone – but especially difficult for someone with agoraphobia.

The psychological condition is marked by an irrational panic-inducing fear of going outdoors.

"I don't like to leave the house and can go for days without actually talking or interacting with anyone," ArLynn tells The ENQUIRER.

The 51-year-old divorcee, mother of two and romance novel writer says that much of the time she can subdue her phobia and go into the world. Her plan to visit Facebook friends was an attempt to conquer her fear completely.

And so, in December 2010, ArLynn began an adventure that took more than a year to complete, as she bravely traveled to 51 cities across the U.S. and to 13 countries around the world. When struck by the inevitable panic attacks, she'd either huddle in a hotel room or rush back home to Winnetka, Ill., and the safety of her comfy chair.

"In the end, you have to spend time with your friends"

**ADDING TO THE TRAUMA OF** international travel, ArLynn also had to deal with the uncertainty of meeting new people. As all Facebook members realize, while some of the people on your friends list are good friends or friends of a friend, others you don't know at all.

"You meet a friend of a friend at a party and you get a Facebook friend request," explains ArLynn. "Most of the time, I click confirm and that's sort of the last I ever hear of the person, except in postings about what they ate for dinner."

For her visits, ArLynn set up meetings via e-mail explaining her pet project. She found most of her friends cooperative. During her year-long journey, agoraphobic ArLynn rode in a motorcycle sidecar, went mountain climbing in California and fished with a health caregiver in Delaware, where she says: "I only caught litter."

She learned how to pop a champagne bottle cork with a Cossack sword, had her face inserted in an Andy Warhol-style print in Mexico, took opera-singing lessons and visited a shrine to cab drivers in India.

In Manhattan, ArLynn visited the Museum of Sex, where Facebook friend Richard "Mop" Furniss works. Through Mop, ArLynn became Facebook friends with Inda Loop, who described herself as a female rapper with huge breasts, great smile and fantastic braids.

"I found out that Inda Loop was really Mop, his other personality, I guess," says ArLynn.

Two of her Facebook friends were pet dogs.

In the end, ArLynn met 292 of her 325 friends. She didn't cure her agoraphobia but learned to be "more forgiving of myself" about having it.

"Facebook is a great tool," she says. "But in the end, you have to spend time with your friends."

by DON GENTILE
dgentile@nationalenquirer.com

A friend gave ArLynn an Andy Warhol look

Music exec/singer John Hill had ArLynn singing like an opera diva

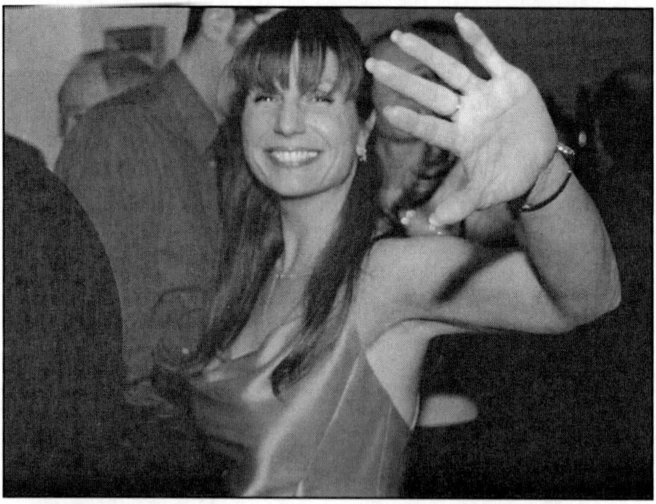

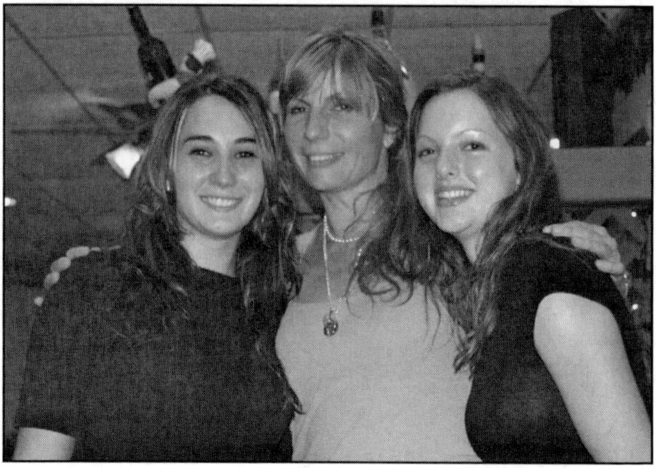

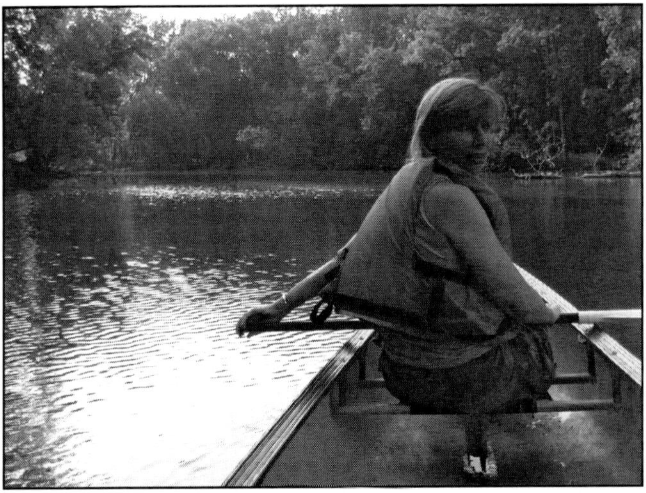

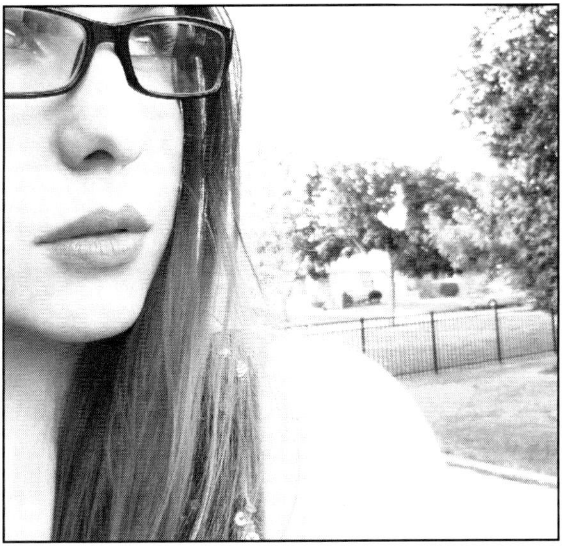

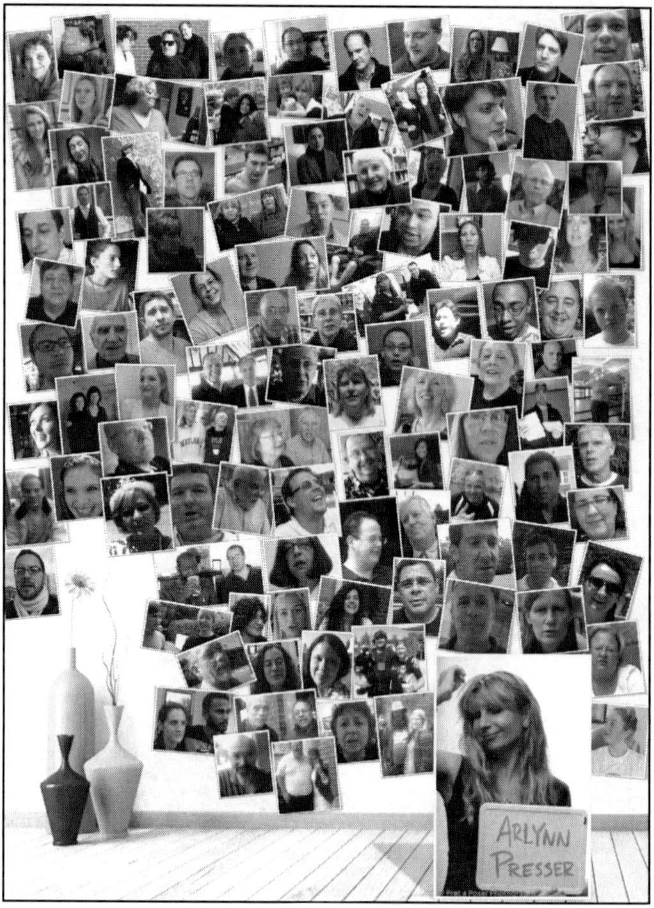
ARLYNN
PRESSER

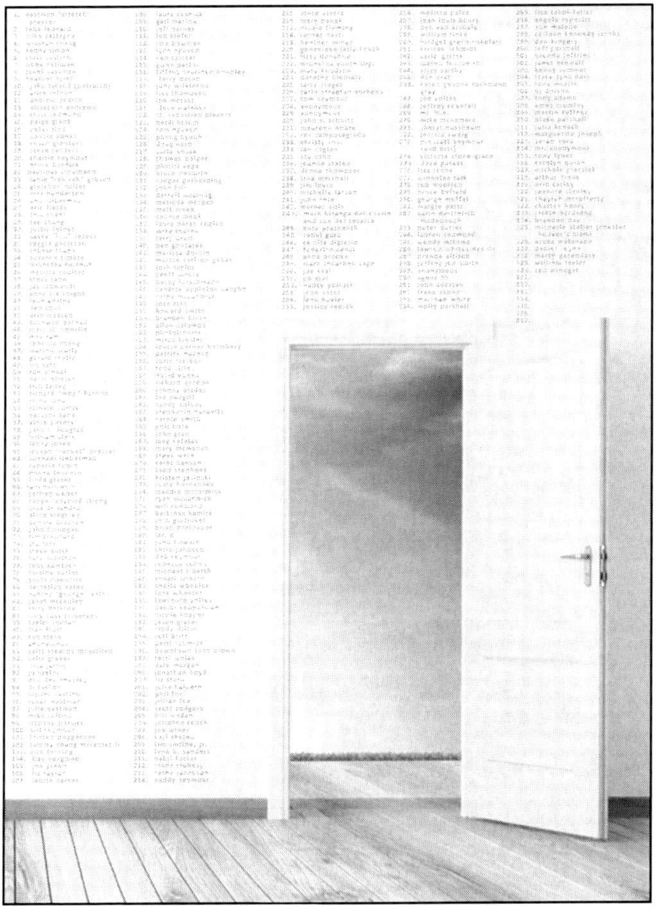

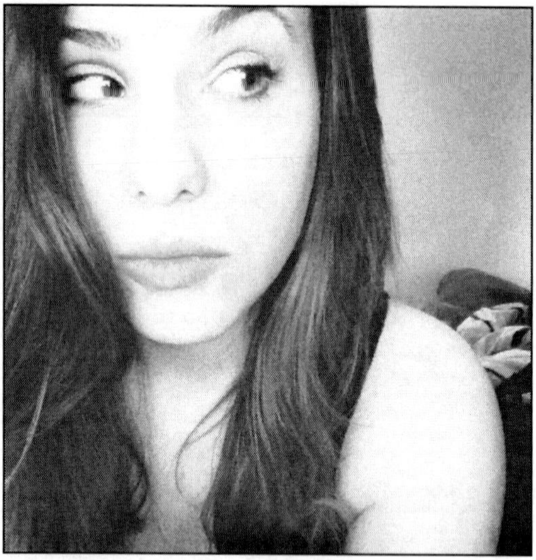
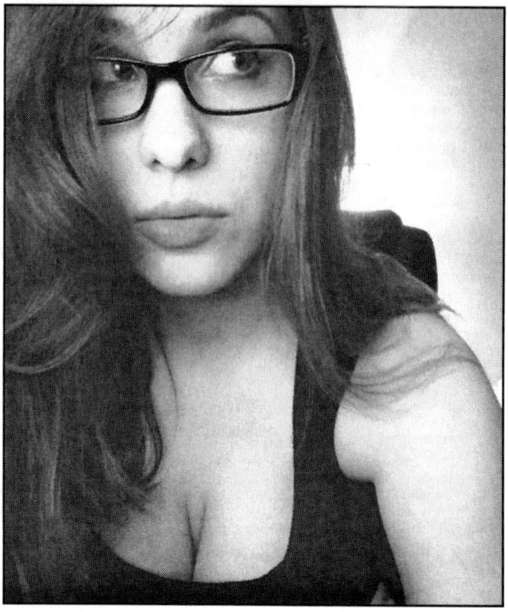